Significance Breeds Success

By Daniel Puder

Significance Breeds Success

www.danielpuder.com

Published by My Life My Power World, Inc.
Printed in the United States of America

ISBN: 979-8-9921239-0-6

This publication is designed to provide accurate and authoritative information in regard to the subject matter covered. It is sold with the understanding that the publisher is not engaged in rendering professional services. If professional advice or other expert assistance is required, the services of a competent professional person should be sought.

Written and Inspired by: Daniel Puder

Writing Support and Edited by: Sheehan Planas-Arteaga

Cover Design: Brittney Lozano @ www.MyLifeMyBrand.com

Significance Breeds Success Dedication

To my parents, Wanda and Brent Puder. You supported me and loved me with all your heart, even when things were hard. Thank you and I love you both.

To my brother, Dr. David Puder, I love you. Thank you for always being supportive and loving no matter what I was doing with my life.

To my son, Konrad Pinto-Puder. I love you. Learn from what I've done, both good and not-so-good. Use this to become the best version of yourself.

To my business partners, Q, Jenn, Brit, Mike, and Ed. Thank you for believing in me throughout this crazy journey. The lessons I have learned that helped make this book a reality were all made possible because of you.

To all of the people who have supported me: Thank you to Dan Salter, Danielle Rosse, Dave Vanhoose, David Heath, David Lawrance, Deborah Reddick, Dr. Mehmet Oz, Ian Moffett, Jamie Manburg, Joe Sauma, John M. Harrington, III, Jose Flores, Luis Marcelino, Marc Kesten, Marc Leder, Mark Ryan, Mayor Karyn Cunningham, Micheal Bargas, Nikki Marie, Ralph Campbell, Dr. Ron Hunter, Dr. Santarvis Brown, Kai Messmer, Stacy Muscleman, Senator Steve Smith, Tammy Pugh, Todd Burns, Trent Steel, Wallace Aristine, Hon. William Chatfield, Joe Tedesco, Kyle Kingsbury, Mark Roy, Alex Lamberg, Hussein AbuHassan, Craig Lee, Dave Levens, Bobby Lopez, Danny Hughes, Ed Connors, Nelson Hincapie, Harlan and Madeline Gittin, Peter Rooney, Frank Shamrock, Javier Mendez, Tom Patti, Jay D'Alba, Harvey Vecherey Scott Manthorne and Jeffery Mitchell.

And a special thank you to Dr. Mehmet Oz and Mike and Kiki Tyson for believing in me.

Want to work for a significant company?
Apply today!

Table of Contents

Afterword by Mike Tyson
COLLEGE of WILLIAM & MARY PUBLICATIONS

Foreword

There's only one Daniel Puder. You hear this type of statement a lot any time someone makes a name for him or herself, but from the first time I met Dan, I knew he was a singular person. Here's a guy who made his living, to put it bluntly, beating people up, then left that world behind at the peak of his powers because he wanted to help underprivileged children and teens by creating a new type of education program: Foundation Academies. And to be clear, he didn't plan on helping these kids by simply writing checks and having someone else go through the trials and tribulations of developing the actual services. Dan was going to leave his fingerprints on every pillar of Foundation Academies, ensuring the company's success.

The concepts Dan preaches in this book, Significance Breeds Success, are something I've always tried to employ in my career. I must say, he hits the nail right on the head. Whatever success means to you, be it financial gain, social status, professional status, a happy home life, etc., you drastically increase your chances of achieving this success when you focus on being as impactful as you can for others. This is exactly why my wife, Lisa, and I founded HealthCorps over 20 years ago. HealthCorps helps underprivileged middle and high school students and young college mentors find success by helping them understand the positive impact they can have on their own health, the health of their families, and their communities. By giving teens the tools to take care of and change their own bodies, they quickly realize they can change the world around them.

I first met Dan at an event centered on National Drug Control Policy. He walked up to me, a mountain of a man, and gave me one of the firmest handshakes I've ever experienced. "My name's Daniel Puder. I'm an undefeated MMA fighter," was his opening line. Then he spoke about what his mission was. What Foundation Academies had already done and what they planned on doing. I understood that Daniel's vision and passion would create opportunity and success for so many who previously did not believe it to be a possibility.

Dan has his sights set perpetually in one direction: forward. He has an uncanny ability to see how industries will evolve, how society will evolve, and how we as people need to prepare ourselves for it. This book not only delves into how one should live a significant life, but how one should adjust accordingly in order to breed success. In this way, Significance Breeds Success represents a multi-faceted boost to any reader seeking a better way to live his or her life. I implore you to participate in all the exercises Dan presents at the conclusion of every chapter. This book is simple, meaningful, and most importantly, useful.

I'm honored Dan asked me to pen the foreword to Significance Breeds Success. I hope you extract as much good out of it as I have.

Mehmet Oz, MD
Professor Emeritus, Columbia University
Founder, HealthCorps

Intro: Finding My Significance

I grew up in Cupertino, California, which is, in my opinion, one of the best and most beautiful cities in the world. I was fortunate enough to have amazing parents who were significant and successful in life, and who gave me a vision of what is possible. I've had my share of ups and downs, which you'll learn about in this book, but as far as my upbringing, I was very lucky.

A little over 13 years ago, I was featured on TMZ for an interesting reason. Most of the time, seeing your face on TMZ, the pop culture breaking news outlet known for having the inside scoop on any and every celebrity scandal, is a bad thing for your career. For me though, it became the catalyst for what has been the most important undertaking of my life.

At the time, I was focused almost exclusively on my career as an undefeated Mixed Martial Arts fighter. I was in my late 20s, had already won WWE's $1,000,000 Tough Enough Championship, and was pursuing another dream of mine, which was to make my mark in the cage as an MMA fighter. This was me at or near my physical peak as a professional athlete.

In other words, addressing bullying and creating solutions for the nation's underserved youth was not exactly at the forefront of my mind. What got me going down this path, however, was reading a social media post shortly before an important dinner. It was related to children and teens committing suicide after being being bullied. I posted on my profile the same day I read this, recounting my own bullying experiences and how this type of story hit close to home. My post got hundreds of responses. I felt the hurt and pain from so many people who went through or were going through something similar.

Then a couple days later, I was out to that dinner I mentioned with one of my mentors. A street interviewer from TMZ named Yori Uehara approached me at the restaurant looking for a soundbite, mostly related to my bullying post, and boy, did I give him one.

Bullying cases were surging in the United States at this particular time, especially for those in the special ed, differently-abled, and LGBTQ communities. When I was asked about this issue in person, I decided to fully insert myself into the conversation.

I offered a solution. Admittedly, a wild one. "Anybody that's getting bullied, in the whole U.S., can shoot me an email. You email me, and I'll go down, I'll fly into a school, and we'll go talk to the bullies for you. I'm dead serious."

I took the opportunity. I put myself out there for a cause I was passionate about and a cause that hit close to home. I was in it now, for better or worse.

Within two months I received over 10,000 emails from parents, adults, and students who had been affected by bullying. Although this was initially about bullying cases in the U.S., these messages spanned 12 countries. My whole life to this point had been about sports, but after seeing how I was able to affect people in the span of one minute in an impromptu interview at a restaurant, I knew I would never be the same.

Helping children and teens who've been dealt a bad hand in one way or another, I now realized, was my opportunity to impact kids' lives, and that was what I was going to do. But how? Where was I to go after the buzz of my TMZ appearance wore off? How would I be able to keep helping young people who were struggling to find success?

I decided to surround myself with a team of educators, law enforcement, mental health experts, and mentorship programs, including the Police Athletic League. My team and I thought the best course of action in the early stages would be to create a youth-based course/book/training module for young adults who could impact the next generation. Then we'd develop a three-tier training system called the Black Belt Program, centered on emotional and belief intelligence. Finally, we'd launch our college-level course and have it implemented at a local university. The school was Nova Southeastern University in South Florida, and the eight-week, three-credit, undergrad course was called GPS for Life®.

Nova Southeastern University agreed to add our GPS for Life® course to their College of Education, on one condition; we had to fill every seat. This presented a challenge. It's not every day a brand new class gets filled up, especially in a school with as many options for students as NSU. Then I had an idea. Why not talk to the athletic coaches to see what they thought about my predicament? Perhaps they'd be able to funnel some of their athletes into our class? For this I sought out Coach Johnson, Nova's head strength and conditioning coach.

I gave Coach Johnson a breakdown of what the class entailed and what it could offer college students, then asked if this was something he thought his student-athletes could benefit from. He responded by saying he felt many players lacked focus and determination. Would a class centered on mentorship, passion, building significance, and emotional and belief intelligence help sort out these issues? Absolutely, he said. And just like that, we were off to the races.

Our GPS for Life® course became filled almost every semester, with a waiting list for some. We decreased the dropout/transfer rate. We focused on building better relationships and understanding ourselves deeper. Most of these students would come back to future classes. They won matches and games with their teams and connected with their families more effectively. I was so proud of the impact we created within this community of young adults and am so excited to see their careers skyrocket in the future. I was hired by NSU with another Adjunct Professor in 2017, which made it easier for me to connect with students, becoming fully engaged with fostering significance, and in turn, success, in their lives.

Around this time, one of my really good friends advised me while I was at an event in Kentucky that I should start my own school system. I thought that was a great idea. I was running around for years working in different systems, putting programs in schools and afterschool programs. This would cause challenges, however. People in different organizations would change positions, and the people who replaced them would often want new programs. I wanted to really impact lives and build a repeatable, sustainable, proven business model. This was only going to be done by building our own schools.

So in 2018, we founded our first school, MLMPI Prep Academy in Liberty City, Florida, and with that, Foundation Academies was born (many of our schools have different names, but they exist under the umbrella of Foundation Academies). Today we have schools in Florida, West Virginia, and Arizona, with plans for rapid expansion within the next few years throughout the United States and internationally. This would not have been possible without my partners and all their hard work, love, and dedication, as well as the innumerable influential people I've met along this crazy ride.

I achieved some significance in the WWE and in Mixed Martial Arts, but it is dwarfed by what I've experienced as an educator. When you pursue significance, as you'll see in the chapters that follow, there is no limit to how successful you can become. It's shocking to think that this phase of my life, in large part, was initiated by that TMZ video. But as they say, small hinges swing big doors. I hope you'll extract value from this book and learn how to live a significant and successful life with fulfillment. Each chapter features self-reflective questions and exercises for you to complete, which I encourage you to make the most of.

We are blessed with only one life to live. Let us choose to live it in the best way possible; by creating significance in ourselves and in our fellow human beings.

Chapter 1: The Power of Perspective

When I was a kid, around middle school age, I took a trip with my youth group to Mexico to build houses. Looking back, this was an experience that taught me something vital: how to help others. Nevertheless, I didn't know the exact meaning of being significant, or how it could affect other areas of my life. There is a major difference between helping people and solving problems. Helping people doesn't necessarily solve issues. I have never heard of a nonprofit putting itself out of business after solving a problem. They help things, sure. But the nature of their business relies upon the problem existing. If it were to be solved, there would be no need for the nonprofit. Our company started as a nonprofit, but we soon learned that the solution to the problems we were facing lay in building a school system.

I'd later realize I went to Mexico to help, not to solve any problems. But it was honest work that taught me some valuable lessons, like the importance of helping others.

When I was in Mexico, I baled hay, helped build homes, and saw a perspective of poverty that I have never experienced in my life. I also observed communities who showed love and commitment, and people who cared and worked hard for their families. The difference between a lower income environment in Mexico and where I was raised in America will really change your perspective on life. The best part of this chapter, and really, Significance Breeds Success as a whole, is you are now taking the red pill of how to love your life. Once you learn what I am about to teach you in this book, and you embrace it, you will become the most fulfilled and at-peace version of yourself, all while obtaining the success you always dreamed of.

I was exposed to a wide variety of perspectives when I was young because of trips like the one I took to Mexico, and this helped me in the early stages of the nonprofit I founded: My Life My Power. At the time, I figured the best way to reach the troubled and underserved youth of this country was through a peer mentorship program. Let's stop telling them what not to do and start inspiring them to follow their dreams. Our main My Life My Power program was called GPS for Life®. We trained mentors, including school police officers, teachers, and afterschool program staff. We also trained the youth they were charged with protecting in order to foster a healthy relationship.

Identifying and Solving Problems

In the beginning of My Life My Power, we looked at what the problem was and tried to address it at its core. But going from school to school was challenging sometimes because a lot of people wanted a speaker to come in, but they did not want to necessarily implement programming or a mentorship curriculum. These things took up a big chunk of hours they were unwilling to dedicate to us. Although I was disappointed in this at the time, today I understand as a private school owner that this type of thing is very challenging due to the lack of time in each school day. I also know that if you fail to plan, your plan is going to fail. Most people we engaged with had a budget for a speaker, though there was no comprehensive plan in place for someone like me to come in consistently in order to become a real catalyst for change. This wasn't anything we couldn't adjust to, however.

We started asking students and parents what their biggest challenges were. The issues were often related to abuse, bullying, a lack of parenting or, conversely, overparenting, and a lack of resources, including food, tutoring, housing, and transportation. Now that we knew the challenges we were facing, the question became, how do we create a program called GPS for Life® and implement this within a school system to make it work for students and parents? For this, I needed the help of an expert like Brittney Sharpe, formerly Brittney Lozano, Edward Davis, and Jennifer Kramer.

We collaborated to create GPS for Life®, but we wanted a deeper understanding of how it was functioning. For this, we hired William & Mary College[1] to conduct studies and be the third party for our Institutional Review Board (IRB), which would tell us how our program was actually doing. Today, we have six published studies to prove that, by implementing our program for one hour per week for five weeks straight, we can increase our youths' value for life through understanding their vision, purpose, mission, team, and improving their sense of commitment. This showed me how to get real results for our youth. We focused on creating value in these young people's lives by reinforcing what they should be doing, as opposed to just what not to do. This was a huge reason why our program worked and this is why our schools work today.

Adding Value

Perspective is vital and can be very simple, yet a lot of us, including myself at times, don't stop to put yourself in somebody else's shoes. I try to acknowledge this challenge every time I talk to kids in Foster Care. I tell them from the beginning that I have no clue what's going on in their lives and, odds are, I haven't experienced anything like it anyway. I grew up with two loving parents and never had to worry about where my next meal was coming from, or where I'd be spending the night. What did I have to offer them? Resources. Relationships. The ability to open doors that they might not have had access

---

1   Excerpts of these W&M publications can be found after chapter 12. To read them in their entirety, visit gpsforsuccess.org/programming/

to coming from where they come from. This was a way I could add value to their lives.

We've seen other people come in and tell them they know what they're going through. They "understand" the struggles. I'd often come to find out afterwards that the person had never been in Foster Care and they were just trying to relate and connect, instead of being authentic with the audience. Perspective is important, but it can't be faked. I challenge people all the time to look at the words they use and the way they live, then consider how they differ from someone with a different upbringing and less resources. How you show up and how you connect with people in this world will give you long-term significance, which breeds your success.

While we were traveling and building a brand, we started striking deals with various law enforcement agencies. We got involved with the White House's National Drug Control policy, which funds the high intensity drug trafficking units. I spoke at different conferences centered on law enforcement, school counselors, and teacher unions. Every of these groups had their own opinions on how to solve the problems facing our underserved youth. One simple truth eventually became apparent to me; no one knew how to solve them. If they did, they would have been solved, or there would have at least been a cohesive plan that everyone was in agreement on.

Most of these challenges require a complex process in order to overcome them, meaning they require a multi-group partnership with comprehensive-rooted solutions. For instance, schools don't necessarily work directly with state or federal education systems and/or with law enforcement to create results in drug prevention. Everybody is doing different things and nothing is being data-tested over longer periods of time, which produces the best information on which to base strategies. These conversations and meetings were intricate. Our main purpose was to simply collect different perspectives from high-ranking people in order to form our own approach and make a difference. Then we'd create the significance millions of kids around the country needed.

The law enforcement agencies were a great network to be a part of because they wanted to impact kids' lives, at least every one we met. The departments we interacted with responded well to our program for this very reason. As someone involved in law enforcement myself, I find the following scenario occurs far too often.

A Police Chief will finish the year having been responsible for getting 100 kilos of illegal drugs off the streets. The following year, he gets 50 kilos off the streets. What does this mean to the mayor and city council, who are largely responsible for him keeping his job? It means he's a failure and is not fulfilling his duty as aptly as he once was. It doesn't matter that the 100-kilo year likely did a ton to prevent a whole generation of youth from ever getting into narcotics. Doing good doesn't always make law enforcement look good. Our program gave them the opportunity to impact future generations, while also improving their perception overall.

The power of perspective gives us the ability to not only help a person today, but to help them build something in the future. This is how we can truly serve the world. When we're attacking these problems, it is vital to not just address a symptom or provide a short-term solution. Perspective allows us to see things from different angles and put the puzzle pieces together more efficiently. Using perspective, we can instead address the root of a problem and provide long-term solutions.

Lauderhill Days

After living in Texas, then Arizona, and subsequently California in the early days of the nonprofit, I made the significant decision to relocate to South Florida. I wasn't alone in this move; two of my business associates, Brittany Sharpe and Eddie Davis, joined me. We settled in Lauderhill, a town in Fort Lauderdale that, at the time, held the reputation of being the 8th most dangerous small city in the country. Despite this, I found the neighborhood to be mostly fine. It wasn't always as easy for my partners, though. Eddie, who has a bit of a swagger to him, and Brittney, a white female standing just five feet tall, attracted more attention than I did.

The following is a brief recounting of our experience in Lauderhill, through Brittney's eyes:

I didn't know it back in 2014, but Lauderhill is not exactly a place you want to be staying for a long period of time. When Daniel pitched us this idea, he mentioned that we would be living in beautiful South Florida with new exciting adventures ahead, not that we'd be woken up nearly every night by the sound of gunshots. Not that we'd be building a barricade of textbooks by the front door, just for a little "added protection" in case a bullet did happen to come flying into our house. Not that Ed would wake up early one morning and walk in the front yard to find a couple of guys in the act of stealing Daniel's tires off his car, leaving it on blocks. Not that we'd be told on several occasions by a police chief to find a new place to stay for the night, because something bad was going to happen on the street where we lived. But in all of the years of my friendship with Daniel (since 2010), I've come to understand that he always has a reason behind the things he does. Living in Lauderhill between 2014 and 2015 was no exception.

Daniel's reasoning was simple and made a lot of sense; if he wanted to be an impactful and significant person in these kids' lives, he had to see how they lived. Or better yet, he had to live among them. I can't tell you how many times Daniel would wake up, go for a walk to the neighborhood basketball court, and simply start making conversation with the kids and teenagers he came across. What is holding you back in your life right now? What do you think your future looks like? What are your goals? That type of thing. He needed to truly understand things from their perspective, as this would make him better at serving them through Foundation Academies.

They always seemed to respond well to him. Ed and I would be busy working behind the scenes while Daniel was the one making impactful connections. It was as grassroots of an effort as there ever was. This was about forming relationships with young people, their families, and the community, all in hopes that they could truly benefit from the mission of Foundation Academies. Daniel was out to break down barriers, and every day he did exactly that.

We started to gain traction as we met with more and more people in South Florida. Similar to our operation in California, we were regularly conducting trainings with police officers and students in order to bridge the gap between them, allowing a means for officers to be seen as mentors and helping create a safer environment that was more conducive to growth in the community. Our ultimate goal was still to start a school system, and after about a year, we opened up our first one.

Six students. One teacher. That was the humble beginning of Foundation Academies. Daniel was in the classroom almost every day helping out in any way he could. He'd pull strings and call in favors to get influential people he knew to come in and talk to our handful of kids, so they could understand what was possible with the right mindset and work ethic. There was no task too big or too small for him, and that approach, from the owner and founder of the company no less, trickled down to all of us.

The time we spent in Lauderhill was full of challenges. It tested each of us mentally, emotionally, financially, you name it. However, sitting here today with schools across multiple states and thousands of students served, I know it was all worth it. That experience and that gained perspective helped build a sturdy foundation for our school system, no pun intended, and it was upon this foundation that we were able to create our significance...and success.

There's no way Foundation Academies would be where it is today without the tireless work of Brittney and Ed in the early days of our company. Perspective is a powerful thing. It keeps us grounded. It makes us appreciative of what we have and how far we've come. I agree with Brittney's analysis of our Lauderhill days. It certainly had its bumps in the road. There were nights when it was natural to wonder if this was all worth it. But we made it. We rolled with the punches and we made it. Apart from the success on the business side that was rooted in these efforts, the perspective we gained in our time in Lauderhill was and is priceless.

Our decision to stay in Lauderhill was scrutinized by people other than Brittney and Ed. Ian Moffett, the Chief of Police for the Miami-Dade School Police Department at the time, visited us a few times. After looking over our situation and our surroundings, he told us flatly that we needed to move. We weren't safe there. Despite this, financial limitations and the will to make a positive impact in this tough neighborhood convinced us to stay for a full year.

I won't say we never had any incidents while we stayed there. Living in Fort Lauderhill meant constant reminders of its crime issues, with frequent sounds of police helicopters and sirens from cars speeding through our streets. Brittney and I both created a process for protecting ourselves and made sure we were aware of our surroundings at all times so that we could get through that year. One time, when Eddie was about to drive a friend to the airport at 4 AM, he discovered two individuals actively removing the wheels from my Scion TC. He yelled, alerting me as to what was happening but by the time I got outside, one tire was already stolen and they were in the process of placing the car on blocks to take the rest. I chased them away and the police came to collect fingerprints, but they never caught the two people who did it.

I did ask law enforcement, if they ever did catch them, to let me know so I could go talk to the judge and maybe mentor them. The police were surprised by this, since those kids had clearly wronged me in this situation. But I am always looking to support people in their growth process, even if they haven't always done right by me. Mental health is the biggest overall challenge based on data in the United States today. What I believe is the core of this issue is value for life. Humans who understand their value and their significance in this world are going to have less mental health challenges and are going to love life on a day-to-day basis. This also means they are less likely to get into trouble; how much they value their own lives will give them more focus to achieve their vision in life.

Liberty City Program

Amid these challenges, we launched an ambitious program aimed at impacting youth in the Miami-Dade area. We managed to introduce our initiative in about 60 schools by collaborating with the Miami-Dade School Police Department. The program connected us with school counselors, assistant principals, or teachers who mentored an average of 10 to 20 kids throughout the year who were going through challenges and needed more mentorship and support. This initiative was incredibly rewarding; I personally visited all the schools and met with the children, witnessing firsthand the positive changes we were initiating.

One particularly memorable moment occurred when we were preparing to start our first program in Liberty City, a neighborhood also known for its high crime rates. While walking through the neighborhood with Commander Carr from Miami City PD, I came across a group of kids playing football. They were having so much fun having one of the older kids throwing the football and acting as all-time quarterback for all the younger ones. As I rounded a corner with Commander Carr, some of the kids said, "Mr. Puder, how are you?" They recognized me from their school where they had participated in our program. Their greeting and sharing about how much they enjoyed our activities reinforced the impact of our work. During this interaction, I asked the kids what they had gained from the program, to which they said that it helped them graduate and improve their lives. This feedback was beyond gratifying and showed me that our efforts were starting to show some significance.

Starting a school in Liberty City was a deliberate choice. We did this to demonstrate the effectiveness of our educational model, which had already shown promising results in other schools, juvenile halls, and even at a university level. What better way to show proof-of-concept than to make a difference in a city with as many at-risk youth as Liberty City? There will be many more stories about how this first school came to be in the chapters that follow.

Fueled By Perspective

Since then, our program has expanded to 11 locations across three different states. By 2024, our Global Corporate Cognia-accredited private school system had successfully graduated over 1,000 students across these states. The friend who originally suggested I start a school will sometimes remind me of his advice with a friendly "I told you so." It's astonishing how a simple suggestion can lead to such significant outcomes. Reflecting on the past six years, I fully agree with my friend that establishing schools has transformed lives more significantly and consistently than any other project I've been involved with. Our nonprofit's work through various programs, training sessions, speaking engagements, social media, and television appearances undoubtedly touched hundreds of thousands of lives. However, the schools have had a deeper, more lasting impact, shaping young individuals' futures by giving them a vision, helping them understand their purpose, and preparing them to live fulfilling lives.

This journey from a dangerous neighborhood in Lauderhill to establishing a transformative educational system across multiple states shows the impact of dedication, community involvement, and belief in the power of significance. No matter how small our beginning was, we had the commitment needed to empower the lives of young people facing diverse challenges. Perspective is an impactful thing to gain as a human being. I find that, the more I learn, see, and experience, the more ability I have to grow as a person. I challenge everybody in their life to go experience something new. For instance, instead of going on a trip to sit on a beach or go to some type of theme park, go serve in a third-world country for a week with your family. See how it changes your perspective. The leisurely vacation will likely make you happier in the short run. But over time,

21

the significance you created for those needy citizens and the perspective you gained as a result of this experience will benefit you more than any sandy beach will. As Americans, we tend to expect certain things that billions of people around the world would consider luxuries. Things like clean drinking water or automobiles or medicines or central air conditioning. One day interacting with people who are different from you will give you all the perspective you need.

And thus, your opportunity to be significant.

Puder's Journal on the Power of Perspective

My challenge to you is I want you to look at a disagreement you have had with somebody else. What was your perspective? Write it down. Then think about what their perspective was. I'm not asking you to be right or wrong, but a lot of people in life love to be right. This will provide a start to your journey of gaining a perspective of other people's situations. It will give you the ability to peer into and live in their world. Developing this skill will also help your leadership abilities grow and make you more effective functioning in a team.

The Disagreement:

_____

_____

_____

_____

_____

_____

_____

_____

_____

Your Perspective:

_____

_____

_____

_____

_____

_____

_____

Their Perspective (Think hard! Reach out to them if necessary.):

_____

_____

_____

_____

_____

_____

_____

How could understanding each other's perspective help reach a mutual agreement?:

_____

_____

_____

_____

_____

_____

_____

Chapter 2: Brick By Brick

Growing up, I was labeled as learning disabled, a label that often paints a pretty bleak picture as to what a student will accomplish in school, especially as it relates to language. Interacting with written words—whether through reading, writing, or editing—posed a huge challenge for me. Much of life is about words and numbers, but these things did not make sense to me. Some days I would go home and just cry on my mother or father's lap because I did not understand the classwork or homework. I didn't know how to learn. And to build something, anything in life, you need to know how to learn. School did not teach me this.

These early challenges, however, made me more resilient and set the stage for a lot of my future business endeavors, including the nonprofit and school system I've already mentioned. These companies required a comprehensive curriculum, a tough task based on my difficulties with language. Thankfully, I had the support of dedicated colleagues like Brittany and Ed, who were each crucial in developing this content. Their assistance was an example of an important lesson that I've carried with me throughout my career: big structures are built using small pieces. Brick by brick. It always requires a comprehensive team effort.

This philosophy of brick by brick became key to my approach as a business owner. If you're an entrepreneur, you are usually starting out with limited resources, meaning you're relying heavily on personal grit. The journey of building a business from scratch, with minimal financial help, can be scary. The effort you have to put in makes it deeply rewarding in the end, though. Think of all the stories of industry giants who started their now-legendary companies in humble settings. For instance, Steve Jobs and Steve Wozniak founded Apple in a small garage in Cupertino, California, and Jeff Bezos started Amazon in a similar garage in Seattle, Washington. Their successes show the importance of some of the irreplaceable elements of running a successful business: time, talent, and treasure.

Of these, I have always valued talent and time the most. I believe the wisdom and skills you develop by beating early challenges can reduce a lot of your future problems. There are so many people who will start a company and raise millions of dollars to fund it in the early going, only to fail and/or give away 90% of their ownership stake. When the money is in their bank accounts, they will often not be as resourceful as they should be.

Figuring out how to be resourceful is a necessity. Every lesson I learned when I had zero dollars in the bank (more on this time of my life later) has taught me how to make better decisions after we become successful. Today's generation wants to be millionaires NOW. Not tomorrow. Not in 20 years. NOW. I believe patience is needed in life in order to promote inner peace.

I pushed myself every day while writing this book with Sheehan Planas-Arteaga, my editor. After one of our sessions, I looked at him after about eight hours, maybe 100 emails and text messages, and thousands of words of written material and said, wow, I didn't get anything done today. This wasn't true, but I have an athlete mindset of pushing myself to my limits. I have learned to let go when I leave the office so that I can be the best father and I'm proud to say I'm able to disconnect nowadays (most of the time). There are some days when I get to take calls until well past midnight, especially when there are reports or project deadlines at stake. More than 90% of the time, however, I get to spend quality time with my family. If you have all the money, fame, or the biggest company in the world, but the ones you love don't have you, then what is it all about?

I urge you to never forget what you're doing all of this for; to be significant and to become the best version of yourself. Not for money. The money comes as a byproduct of focusing on what's important.

Learning the Ropes

I have a great memory of my childhood when I assembled a remote-controlled race car and an innovative squirt gun I called the "water otter." These projects, though simple, taught me the principles of being hands-on with a project, which is vital for building a successful business. These values are missing in a ton of modern educational curriculums, sadly, even those that claim to focus on entrepreneurship. In the 2024 school year, we will have an entrepreneurship course for all of our students at Foundation Academies, and it will create a ton of opportunities for practical experience that our kids can use to develop their skills. I would encourage students to learn the basics of starting and running a business, from registering the company, to understanding personal and business credit, to actually selling a product and generating revenue. This is what your teens and early adulthood should be about: exploring, growing, learning, and being mentored. I believe when you get into your 30s, you should focus on what you are doing and build upon the relationships you formed in your 20s. By 40, you should have a really good foundation for your career.

The start of my career in entrepreneurship was significantly shaped by the relationships I had, particularly with Michael Williams, whose partnership in Foundation Academies began in a unique way, a way that shows how two people with two very different backgrounds can come together for a shared vision. This connection was built on our shared commitment to invest not just money, but time and expertise into this dream. These collaborations have been key to the creation and growth of Foundation Academies, which now offers a wide range of services, from security to education to health. Each of these addresses specific community needs.

When it came to growing my businesses, my goal was always to be as independent as possible. I wanted to build this thing with nearly zero investments from third parties, in order to avoid giving up equity in the company. This approach required a lot of time and energy from me and my committed partners like Mike. We wanted to show that time, energy, and grit could actually be more valuable than just collecting a ton of investments up front. Over time, this model has worked, allowing us to create a multi-million dollar revenue stream, support over 140 staff members, and continually reinvest in Foundation Academies.

Despite this success, the process of building a business brick by brick requires more than just effort; you need to get over operational challenges, which means you yourself must be able to do the industry-specific tasks, or you need to find the right people to handle things for you. This includes drafting detailed business plans, creating financial forecasts or marketing initiatives, or directly recruiting and training staff. Each step involves a hands-on approach. In the early days, this meant me and a few other people doing things like interviewing potential employees to ensuring our facilities met every compliance requirement. You need to be ready to be a jack of all trades in the early stages of your business.

The term "brick by brick" captures the concept of building something significant from the ground up, not only in the literal sense, but also through planning and execution. Partners of mine like Guillermo Queris and Jennifer Kramer have supported me in fulfilling this strategy. Their insights have been invaluable. Together with the support of my mother, a public school teacher, and other educational professionals, we have gotten over both the educational and business pitfalls of our industry in order to create value and solve complex problems.

Throughout this book, I'm going to dive into some of the challenges of Foundation Academies along this journey. It is important for young entrepreneurs to understand that success often follows a ton of trials and errors. Sharing these experiences is about showing you the resilience, adaptability, and strategic thinking you need to get over obstacles and achieve lasting significance.

Getting to Know Mike

Brick by brick. That was always our mentality. Mike Williams is one the core partners of Foundation Academies, and one of a handful of people who knows how challenging it was in the early stages of our company. The following excerpt is his account of some of the mountains we had to scale while getting Foundation Academies off the ground:

I first met Dan a decade ago, when I was running a juvenile residential facility in Kendall, a suburb of Miami. When I tell you I was wrong about this man, it's a gross understatement. You have to understand, in my line of work I've seen hundreds of people walk through the door talking about how they're going to change these kids' lives through this program or that program. After a short while, they'd run out of steam. They'd talk the talk, but weren't willing to walk the walk when it came to troubled youth reform.

I thought Dan was cut from the same cloth as these other folks. He had little to no experience dealing with kids in this situation, and had almost nothing in common with them: race, upbringing, interests, nothing. When he walked into our residential center laying out a plan to get the inmates the help they needed and asking to go inside and interact with them, I thought he was exactly like the rest of them. Nice words. Good intentions, but nothing to back it up.

I told him he could not come speak to our kids and tried to get rid of him. He convinced me to give him just one day with 30 minutes of sharing his story with the kids. Telling them what he is up to in life and how he got there. I let him, not thinking he was capable of much. I was thinking the kids would take care of kicking him out for me. "You want to help these kids?" I asked. "Sure thing, go talk to them and see how it goes." This would either prove to me that he was worth my time, or it would scare him away. I allowed him to go speak to the general population of our residential center.

You'd usually see plenty of action when our residential center members all got together. After letting Dan in, I noticed there were no fights, screaming, or general disruptions going on. It had been a while, and all I heard was peaceful discussions. I went and took a look for myself and could barely believe my eyes; Dan had them sitting in a circle, which he stood in the center of. Talking about life's obstacles and how to overcome them and plan for the future. It took a lot for us to get that kind of cooperation and interaction from our population. For Dan to get it in just a few hours was no small feat. I was impressed. He asked me if he could come back and I told him yes and do the same thing if he wanted, and he did.

The man just kept coming back, though. Dan would march in with a head full of big ideas and infinite optimism and energy.

Every time he'd speak to our kids, he just brought himself. This made his actions even more impressive. He didn't need to offer them candy or any sort of treats for them to behave. It was his message and his presence that took care of them. The energy he brought into the room drew everyone to him. What's this big guy got to say? And, he kept coming back.

One interaction in particular got me to commit to Dan's brand and program once and for all. When any inmate of ours was released, it was often my custom to ask and talk to them about their future plans. What are your plans once you're free again? You're getting older, you have to make smarter decisions. What will you do for money? That type of thing. Just to reinforce it in their minds that they should not renew the bad habits that got them in here in the first place. One kid in particular starts laying out a timeline of how he's going to be successful, complete with dates, objectives, strategies, the whole nine. I was shocked. "How'd you come up with all this?" I asked. From Daniel Puder, that big blonde white guy he said. "Did he tell you to say this?" I followed with. No, the boy said, and that Dan's discussions had inspired him to create a plan for how he was going to improve his life. He mentioned the five major topics I taught: vision, purpose, mission, team, and commitment.

That was it for me. After those open meetings at our residential center and the effect I saw it was having on our kids, I needed to see Daniel Puder in action outside our walls.

He told me he was teaching a class at Nova Southeastern University up the road, and that I should stop by to learn about the course: GPS for Success. Similar to the detention center, people were always engaged with the messages he was delivering. I also loved the content of the course and thought it could be useful for anyone, not just for college students. I realized that Dan and I, although from completely different backgrounds, had a ton in common. What he had that I didn't have, however, was the people skills and presence necessary to break down the doors on the way to this goal. Dan and I were on the same team.

I showed up to the Nova Southeastern University course. Throughout the night, from 4:00 to 8:00 PM, Dan and the other professor would lead these young adults in this three-credit course using experiential learning. It was the first time in my life I saw experiential learning at this level of schooling. Now, I have a Masters Degree; I've been around the block. But what stood out to me with this group was that each one of these students loved bonding and connecting with each other. They were not afraid to speak up or talk about who they were and what they wanted, and they were creative and thinking outside of the box. At one point in the night Daniel had them all doing a dance. A dance! College kids! He asked me if I wanted to come up and dance with the group. I looked at him and said, "no thank you," from the back of the room. I will admit though, after watching these students having fun I started moving around a little. I ended up partaking in this dance a bit.

He supported each one of them by getting them out of their shells, opening up, and feeling accepted for who they were and what sort of dream they were chasing. It's no wonder Dan became one of the highest ranked professors on ratemyprofessors.com while at NSU.

The purpose of this entire ordeal, for us, was to create a platform to stem the tide of young people committing crimes and feeding an ever-expanding industrial prison complex.

The way to do that was to do exactly what I saw him do in my facility; teach these young people about values, purpose, vision, and belief intelligence. We tried many options, including partnerships with the Dept. of Education, police departments and other civic institutions, but none could fit us in because of "budgetary constraints." The concept of opening a school was born out of the realization that we were going to have to do this on our own.

Dan came to me with the idea of launching our first school in Liberty City, along with an after-school program for foster care youth in South Miami. I told him right away that I was in, and we hit the ground running. Maybe running is the wrong term. It was more of a sprint and stop. Sprint and stop, sprint and stop. The plan was to open a school for underserved youth and to offer them an alternative curriculum that could help them graduate and evolve as people. But we needed a location. So we went, literally, door to door looking for a serviceable building that could support our students, which we did not have any of yet. To make the absolute most of our time, we would literally run from building to building, then compose ourselves and give our best pitch. Hence, sprint and stop.

We tried libraries. We tried churches. We tried city park centers. If it met the codes and was in a neighborhood that needed a school system like us, we were making our pitch. After miles and miles and days and days of leg work, Dan and I finally found our first location: a classroom at the African-American Cultural Arts Center in Liberty City. The classroom was as bare bones as you can imagine. A chalkboard and a few old desks and chairs. That's all. But it was a classroom and it was ours to use. That was all that mattered. Now all we needed was some students!

We set out to pitch our idea to as many parents as possible. Dan and I would set up our table at the Cultural Arts Center, complete with fliers and pamphlets with a general overview of our concept. It was not easy to break through to these people. Not because our ideas were bad, but because we had no proof of concept. We'd never done this before and had no way of ensuring these parents that their kids were in good hands. All we had was a good idea and all we could ask for was a little faith. This is not something people just hand out, so it was difficult to enroll our first student. But not impossible.

One student finally signed up. Then two. Then three. We were getting an itty bitty bit of traction, but we still needed help paying the bills. Grant money from another contract that we worked on would help do that for us, and we were able to secure one by running an afterschool program in Homestead, Florida, which is about an hour south of Liberty City. An hour and a half if there's traffic. This meant a ton of mileage put on my SUV. Eventually, disaster struck.

I totaled my vehicle. A ton of driving finally got the best of me and I wrecked on my way home from our afterschool program. I wasn't seriously injured, thankfully. But the SUV was done for. I needed a new way to get around. Dan had a great idea; get a Prius.

Dan drove a Prius at the time. I always chuckled to myself seeing this 6'3", 250-lb former mixed martial arts fighter climb out of a Prius, but when it came to traveling long distances on a tight budget, this was a great option. I didn't have the funds at the time, so Dan took care of it. I now had a more reliable, affordable option to commute from Liberty City to Homestead to whatever meeting or event we were set to go to.

We enrolled 17 students by the end of our first year in business. Knowing what we went through to get here, and seeing Dan in action up close, indicated to me that this idea was worth sticking with. This was certainly not a lucrative operation yet; I had to do some convincing with my family when I told them

I wanted to embark on this journey, because I wasn't going to be bringing in much money in the beginning. But I believed in Dan and I believed in Foundation Academies. We were going to build this thing up piece by piece. Our other partners Guillermo Quest and Jennifer Kramer along with Britney Lozano and Eddie Davis all spent a lot of time and effort every single day making sure these operations ran smoothly.

Like I said, my first impression of Daniel Puder was very wrong. I'm infinitely grateful to have met this man. No hurdle or challenge is going to stop him from achieving his vision for life, or from continuing to grow our company, Foundation Academies.

The first time I met Mike, he was impacting kids in juvenile hall, but unfortunately, didn't trust me to try to do the same with his troubled youth. Fast forward to now, and his expertise, wisdom and skill set was just as valuable as mine in the early days of our school system. He also trusts me now, thankfully!

Mike and I both knew it would take hard work, sweat, and some tears in order to get this thing off the ground, especially without any major donors pushing us forward. But we did it, as shown by our 11 locations across three states, with plans for major expansion over the next few years. My goal is to reach a thousand locations across the country and internationally in order to impact more youth than any other school district. We'll do this by embracing and understanding the future of technology and how each community is moving forward. We can use data to design the highest level of education, customized for each outcome, which will support communities in the future. This will then inspire and elevate our educational system around the world.

Brick by brick was always the way to go for me, even if it took us longer than it might've with the help of investors. When you build a company the way we did, it often feels more significant and meaningful, as opposed to relying heavily on investors in the beginning. This has fueled us to seek out and achieve significance for thousands of families who needed it. The success has followed, and the success will continue to follow.

This is how we do things at Foundation Academies.

Puder's Journal about Brick by Brick

When creating your vision in life, I want you to think about how you piece each brick together to get the results you want. Take one thing you're doing today that you're maybe having some challenges with. Write down your vision below, then work backwards from there.

My challenge for you is, if you don't know how to achieve this goal, call three to five people and pick their brains. If you want to become a lawyer, for instance, and you don't know what type of law you'd like to practice, my advice is to call three to five law firms and simply ask about the nature of their professions. I'd also research hourly demands, how much revenue they produce and take home, what it looks like to have your own law firm, etc. Google is a powerful tool and so are AI platforms like ChatGPT. Use them, collect the data you need, and start building something brick by brick!

What is your challenge today?:

_____

_____

_____

_____

List the steps to take towards achieving your vision:

_____

_____

_____
_____
_____
_____
_____
_____
_____
_____

What can you do to achieve that goal today/this week?:

_____
_____
_____
_____
_____
_____
_____

Write down all results from your research and efforts here:

_____
_____
_____
_____
_____
_____
_____
_____
_____
_____
_____

Chapter 3: Significance Through Failure

This chapter is a misnomer right off the bat. I do not believe in failure. Those who know me know I try to never say I failed at anything in life. There are two options whenever I approach a new endeavor.

Option 1: I succeed. I smash it. Everything is great and I can move onto the next mountain to climb.

Option 2: I learn. I did not produce the result I originally wanted for myself and/or Foundation Academies, but that's ok. Because instead, I have gained valuable knowledge about how I can succeed at this same task in the future.

This is a valuable mindset to have as a business owner. When I launched my first company as a kid, it didn't work. Same with the second idea, and the third idea. Most successful entrepreneurs get about 90% of what they do wrong the first few times around. But no one sees these on their résumés or LinkedIn.

People often operate in a succeed/fail system. Whatever goal they're shooting for, no matter how big or small, can be boiled down to succeeding or failing. Winning or losing. You either accomplish what you set out to do, or the whole thing was a failure. This mentality can be harmful. In life, especially as you get older and the tasks get more difficult, you'll find that success becomes more of a process. Foundation Academies has now impacted thousands of lives across the country. But it took a lot of learning to get there. Not failures. Learning experiences. You know what these learning opportunities taught us how to do? **Be more significant.**

Anyone who is significant has had successes, but success doesn't mean you are significant. I've had plenty of moments as a professional athlete and business owner that I was focused on the money or the personal outcome more than providing value for someone else. Now I know that when we focus on significance, more success follows in its wake.

Embracing Mistakes

In this chapter of my life, I've come to rethink what many might label as failure. It's not a dead end, like it might seem, but an essential part of learning and succeeding. Others who clearly had this perspective on things include people like Thomas Edison and Elon Musk, whose careers show that breakthroughs usually come after coming up short over and over again (all opportunities for growth). Edison famously tested thousands of materials and designs before perfecting the light bulb as we know it today. He was effectively discovering what did not work as opposed to what did, something he could have easily misconstrued for failing.

Similarly, Musk invested all his resources into SpaceX, knowing well that repeated launch mishaps could have spelled the end for his companies. These stories show that failure is not about falling short but about gaining the knowledge you need to adjust your approach. Here, I will share how facing and overcoming my challenges have taught me invaluable lessons and defined my approach to life and success.

My struggles in the classroom began early. Since I was diagnosed as learning-disabled, I was placed in special education classes in elementary school. In the traditional schooling system, which is built only for certain learning styles, I struggled a ton. The system demanded quiet, long periods of concentration, something that was pretty much impossible for me as a hyperactive child. My son, Konrad, has similar energy levels as I did at his age, but I see how little has changed in schooling, unfortunately.

Flawed Systems

Many school districts offer minimal time for physical activity, which is crucial for children like Konrad, who need to expend energy in order to focus. Countries like Finland, Sweden, and Switzerland offer better solutions for students with different learning styles, as their education systems integrate physical activity with learning.

In Finland, kids start pre-primary education at six years old, and compulsory school at seven years old. In 2020, they were number one in the world in various education metrics, as rated by the Worldwide Educating for the Future Index (WEFFI)[2]. So why are millions of other children failing when they can read, write, and know basic numerical functions when they are four or five years old?

I love Finland's approach. I take note of my son at three-and-a-half, asking us to read to him, asking what a sign means, or if we can teach him this or that. A mindset in which you are willing to learn, grow, and think is powerful compared to a mind that gets robbed of this will, which I believe is what happens in educational systems like ours. Pushing students because of their age, which comes with a huge range of maturity depending on the child, is not the right way to do things in my opinion. Each person learns at his or her own pace. Help foster a growth mindset and you will create someone who wants to learn.

At one point, in an effort to help me concentrate, my doctors prescribed pharmaceuticals, a common practice for handling energetic kids. This does not address the root of my

---

[2] Data from OECD.org

issue, though. Instead, they made me feel like crap and I did not stay on them for long. These experiences in school made me feel like a failure, incapable of succeeding in a traditional learning environment. This thought pattern got even worse when, halfway through the eighth grade, I was nearly expelled from a private school due to my inability to meet their academic and behavioral expectations.

My parents and I decided to transfer back to the public school system, where I continued to struggle, especially with mathematics. I vividly remember the teacher who failed me, which was one of the lowest points in my career as a student. And yet, I was still sent to the next grade each year, even though I clearly wasn't ready for more complicated material. This reveals another flaw in a system more concerned with moving students along than ensuring they learn.

It was safe to say I wasn't destined to be a top scholar. However, my journey took a turn in college when I began to understand my learning style. I discovered that constant activity, such as taking detailed notes and maintaining a balanced diet and hydration throughout the day in each class, helped my cognitive function. A few of my teachers asked why I brought food to class. I told them I needed to keep my body working. These strategies not only helped me improve my grades, but also gave me the tools to succeed in professional settings. I use these techniques to this day.

Life's Ups and Downs

This mindset of failures being learning opportunities was crucial as I entered the professional world, particularly when it came to combat sports. It tested my physical and mental limits daily, and in the beginning, I had way more losses in training than I did wins. Each session, however, taught me more about perseverance, strategy, and resilience. There was a reason I lost. My only job after it was over was to analyze how and why it happened, then figure out how to prevent it from happening again. Mixed martial arts comes with no shortage of struggles, in and out of the cage.

One of the most trying times of my life came when I was 26, trapped in an exclusive fight contract that stalled my career. Despite being ready and eager to compete, I was sidelined by the promotional company's inaction. The struggle to find a lawyer willing to challenge this on a contingency basis, coupled with rapidly running out of money, pushed me to the brink. Eventually, after much effort finding a lawyer to help me learn about contracts, I was able to get out of it. In the process, I had gained a deep understanding of legal strategies and the importance of understanding binding agreements. These lessons were tough, but valuable.

These experiences have affected my approach to failure and success. Every setback, every challenge, and every apparent failure has the potential to teach us something valuable if we let it. Whether it's fixing an invention like Edison, saving a rocket launch like Musk, or getting through the educational system and breaking free from constrictive fight contracts like I had to do, the lessons learned from these experiences are what drive us forward.

Looking back on this rough time in my life I see several ways it could be looked at as a personal failure. My understanding of contracts at the time was very basic, a common scenario many companies use to take advantage of athletes. This is a widespread issue in the sports industry, where managers and agents often have to manage the interests of many athletes, which sometimes leads to neglecting their individual needs due to bigger commitments with sporting companies. During this time, my agent and coach chose not to back me, and ultimately, I had to cut ties with both of them. I would approach things differently if I had the knowledge and resources I have now. Was it a failure? No. But that doesn't mean I wouldn't change anything if I could go back, especially to the time when I signed the contract in the first place.

This whole ordeal felt like a mountain I couldn't climb. Though it lasted about 12 months, my extreme money issues forced me to think creatively about earning a living. The emotional toll was heavy; many nights ended in tears, and there were days I wished I could simply sleep away the frustration and stress. Handling this battle alone was daunting and put my resilience to its limits, more so than anything that ever happened in the ring.

One of my biggest mistakes was not knowing the right questions to ask or who to turn to for help. There are critical skills everyone should master, and one of them is how to find solutions when there's a problem you can't solve. I didn't have enough of these skills at the time, sadly. A particularly low moment was when I had to surrender my dream car, a black on black Nissan 350Z, 35th Anniversary Edition, which got repossessed. I had the option to ask a local mentor of mine, whom I thought of as a second father, for help. He could have easily helped me manage the payments or secure a less expensive vehicle. But my pride or ego prevented me from seeking him out. I regret not doing that, and it took me a while to understand these lessons. I tell you my hardships so that you will not repeat the same things I did.

This chapter of my life was full of struggles, but was also a huge learning experience. It taught me the importance of understanding legal and financial documents, having trustworthy representation, and the value of humility in asking for help. I've taken these lessons and processed them to become a wiser, more prepared person in both my professional and personal life.

To anyone facing their own challenges, let me give you this little piece of advice: embrace them. This approach will transform the way you tackle problems by redefining failure as just a simple part of the learning process. When our "failures" end up becoming positives due to the knowledge we gain because of them, we are much more likely to excel in whatever field we're in. With this mindset, nothing can beat us.

Down, Never Out

I now view failure not as a misfortune, but as a mindset.

Often, people look at failure as something that happens to them, which can lead to a victim mentality. I'll be the first to admit I let this mentality creep in when I was going through my contractual issues as a fighter. However, if your mind is trained to see this natural part of life as an opportunity for growth instead, you have no reason to feel victimized. Although my problems outside the ring sometimes got the better of me, I always had the ability to use a more constructive approach when I was in the ring.

Like I said earlier, pretty much every training session when I first started training with professionals was a defeat. I was being punched, kicked, and thrown around by the best fighters in the world at American Kickboxing Academy, all of whom were more experienced fighters. It was like a high school football player stepping directly into the NFL, facing off against the most seasoned professionals. These guys were relentless. None of them wanted to be beaten by a 17-year-old. But still, I was never defeated. Each fight made me better, no matter the result.

By the age of 19 or 20, this perspective started to pay off. The fighters who used to dominate me were now the ones I was taking down. I remember a specific session around this time when I continually took down one of my training partners, which frustrated him. He complained to our coach, unable to get himself out of my holds on his own. This moment told me a lot; it's not about the setbacks themselves, but how we respond to them. I knew right then he was not as strong as I was and his focus and emotions were not as controlled in a fight environment. I knew I could beat him not because of any physical advantage, but because I was focusing on being the best version of myself.

I was learning to feel, learning to understand pain with each training session. But I would not let the opponent know what was going on, in order to fuel my advantage. I now know that, in life, there are times to be tough and times to be vulnerable and open. But when I was young, I did not understand how to get through tough times without being tough. Looking back, I should have helped this person get over his issues in the ring.

I focused on learning and adapting from each encounter I had with a training partner. This mindset transformed what could have been seen as failures into stepping stones towards victories. There's no way to understate how important our perception is of difficult times in life. A person who uses challenges as fuel is someone who is basically guaranteed to be successful.

I think about a story I have heard over and over again, and it goes like this. Strong people create easy times, easy times create weak people, weak people create hard times, hard times create strong people once again. I think about our lives in the United States and compare it to countries with far less fortunes than us, but with more love and a tougher spirit, based on what I've observed in my travels. They can go without the resources, money, or food and live in some of the most challenging situations on Earth, while still being happy.

I think to myself, if I did not have these hard times, these challenges, then who would I be today? Would I be a more successful fighter? Perhaps. But would I want that life? Would it be better than what I've built since then? I am so blessed to be where I am and with the people I am around, including my partners, family, and friends, all working towards impacting at-risk youth. I also think about my son, how I need to love him while also challenging him. I have come to the conclusion that the more I love him, show him the world, support his creativity, and push him in the things he is interested in, while keeping him accountable to his commitments, the more he is on track to become a significant leader in this world. These lessons and this life I've built would not have been possible without the hardships I went through early on.

Addressing Challenges

In 2010, I embarked on a significant journey to start a nonprofit aimed at transforming the lives of young people through motivational speaking, educational programs, and training. This path, filled with goals to make a profound impact, was more challenging than I thought. My early attempts to connect with people often missed the mark—I struggled to move the crowd, book events efficiently, and genuinely impact both the children and adults in front of me. Repeatedly, I encountered dismissive reactions; so people would simply walk away, leaving me to question if this was the right approach at all.

I was trying to look at the root of the issues and help kids figure the solutions out themselves. A simple example is that most adults and school staff teach their students concepts like "no bullying." Well, there are two issues with this approach. One, if the word "Don't" or "No" is prominent in your lesson and you focus on what not to do without explaining the right way to do things, the students will have a worse understanding of the proper behavior. The second issue is when you talk about bullying, drugs, gang-related activities, etc. you focus on the negative things going on versus helping kids fulfill themselves and create value in their lives. That only happens when the students understand their vision and purpose for being on this Earth: to become significant and impactful in people's lives.

Most of the schools we were working with or nonprofit organizations just wanted us to talk about bullying, mainly related to the negative effects of it. It's simple to explain why somebody bullies another person, and my go-to encapsulating phrase is this: hurt people hurt people and loving people love people. I believe when people have a higher level of emotional intelligence and belief intelligence, their hearts and minds work to create results that are in alignment with their vision.

At several events, when we did manage to engage with the audience, we brought along books and discussed our programs, proclaiming their potential to transform lives. Despite our enthusiasm, the response was sometimes less than we expected. Schools would tell us they didn't have the time to incorporate our programs, which aimed to change the students' mindsets. This resistance was tough to handle, especially since most of the educators we talked to said the same thing.

At one event in Southern California, children shared some pretty troubling personal stories—one talked about being hit by his father for getting a B, and another told a story about an incident when his father broke his own foot on his face while kicking him. These stories deeply affected us and once again showed me the desperate need for change not only within families, but also within the educational systems that failed to address these issues.

We needed to adapt and enhance our methods if we were to make any meaningful impact. We started collecting feedback and seeking insights from external experts who could offer fresh perspectives on our challenges. This new approach allowed us to understand different communities' needs and improve our strategies. It was hardship and pressure due to not getting things right that made us grow. If two people go to the gym and do the same workouts, many times, one will quit and one will take the struggle and use it to progress. Significance helps every person get through the harder times, because if you're doing it to live out your vision and purpose in life, you will have the necessary grit and focus when the going gets tough.

As humans we become what we spend the most time doing. If you want to become an athlete, spend time training every single day. If you want to become an educator, go to college and study how to educate others. Similarly, if you want to become an amazing human and the best version of yourself, work on your mind and your heart every single day.

In many of today's schools, they build the educational system around reading and memorizing content in order to then take standardized tests. This is why there is a new movement called school choice in a lot of the states around the country, which allows parents to not be restricted by the area they live in when making decisions about which school their child will attend. Do they really want them sitting for eight hours a day learning to regurgitate what they see on a screen or board? The tide is turning and more progressive educational systems will win out. More and more states will offer school choice in the next 10 to 20 years. Competition breeds improvement, and the fact that schools will have less of a guaranteed enrollment will force them to adapt in order to improve with the times. People want to have the choice of where they send their kids to get educated.

Parallels in Combat Sports

Similar to the challenges with my nonprofit, I faced some pretty steep mountains in my professional wrestling career, particularly during my time with WWE, which many considered a failure. However, I viewed this period as a crucial learning phase. Before entering WWE, a mentor and good friend, Ed Connors, advised me to make dramatic changes—bleach my hair, develop a six-pack, and tan. His guidance was a reminder of how one individual's advice could significantly impact someone's career path.

Despite my passion for professional wrestling, I encountered numerous hurdles, including a particularly tough coach during the WWE Tough Enough Challenge. This coach pushed the boundaries of traditional training; he once even bent my finger back during a drill to the point where it nearly broke, just to prove a point. I looked at him and said I'm here to learn and grow, but if you're going to break my finger, just do it. There's a fine line between tough guidance and risking an athlete's health, and this was one of the first coaches I had who showed me where that line was.

This is not to say everyone I met in the WWE was like this. During Tough Enough, my other coach, Al Snow, taught me a valuable lesson; it is better to be respected and disliked versus liked and not respected. He was proud of how I showed up, worked my butt off, listened, and learned to the best of my ability.

These experiences in wrestling were a lot like the lessons I was learning through my nonprofit work—both arenas taught me the value of resilience, proper technique, and the importance of adapting to overcome challenges. At the

American Kickboxing Academy under Javier Mendez, I learned invaluable lessons about hard work, grit, and the importance of teamwork. He taught me that, even in areas most people see at individual efforts, like MMA or wrestling, support from others who are going through the same challenges is crucial for personal achievement and overall success.

The concept of teamwork extended beyond the ring and into every aspect of my nonprofit endeavors. Working together enhances individual performance and strengthens the entire organization, leading to long-term success and a supportive environment. I've seen how organizations with self-centered attitudes can stunt growth and create a toxic atmosphere. On the contrary, when you have a culture that emphasizes support and collective success, the company thrives as each team member thrives. You end up creating something people want to be a part of.

Reflecting on these experiences, it's clear to me that using perceived failures as opportunities to learn, embracing change, and creating a teamwork culture are very important for personal and professional growth. Each challenge faced by the nonprofit and each setback I had in the wrestling ring or MMA cage was not a stumbling block but a stepping stone to improvement. Using this perspective has driven me and made me constantly strive for excellence, while also helping others rise above their circumstances.

Puder's Journal on Significance Through Failure

I want you to think about how you look at failure. Down below, make a conscious choice to not look at failure in life as a byproduct of you not being good enough, smart enough, etc. Instead, look at failure as a lesson in life. This gives you the opportunity to learn from it to become the best version of yourself and achieve great things.

What is a "failure" you've experienced?

_____

_____

_____

_____

_____

How could you have looked at this "failure" differently?

_____

_____

_____

_____

_____

What lessons have you now learned and how will they help you become more significant?

_____

_____

_____

_____

_____

Chapter 4: Selfless Significance

Choosing a life dedicated to significance is a profound decision, often motivated by the desire to contribute to the lives of others. This choice is on display in professions like police officers, firefighters, and military personnel, but it extends far beyond these roles. The core of selfless significance is about making a difference, often without expecting any sort of reward. Those who commit to this path usually find that the act of giving gives them immense internal rewards, like fulfillment, love, and inspiration. These benefits might not show in material wealth like lavish houses or luxury cars, but they improve the giver's mental health, attitude, and personal growth over time. The principle of selfless significance can be applied in any professional setting, from fast food services, to nonprofit organizations, to education positions. People who adopt this mindset often find themselves achieving the highest levels of personal development, and quickly too. They become the best versions of themselves by supporting and uplifting their families, friends, communities, and workplaces.

A lot of times, the drive to give back is rooted in personal experiences. For example, people who work with abused women may have faced similar challenges themselves, and those who assist in drug rehabilitation might have battled addiction. Having lived through these things, they are uniquely positioned to understand and connect with others facing similar struggles. This deep empathy allows them to make a significant difference.

Many of my friends who now dedicate themselves to helping others have overcome difficult pasts. Their efforts in supporting groups they identify with is driven by a deep understanding of the challenges these people face. The connection stems from their own journeys of recovery and personal development. By giving back, they not only help others heal but also continue to heal themselves, creating relationships based on shared experiences.

Ultimately, living a life centered on helping others isn't just about the acts of service performed; it's about fostering a sense of connection and community. It's about changing weakness into sources of strength, both for yourself and others. This is transformative. It allows people to grow alongside those they are helping. Everyone involved ends up becoming more understanding and empathetic versions of themselves.

Significant Friends

Throughout my life, I have been fortunate to encounter individuals who embody the spirit of selfless significance, but this was not blind luck. I have made a point to connect with like-minded people when it comes to significance. I chased what I have today by creating value for others. These people have impacted my path and have also demonstrated how transformative and fulfilling it is to live a life dedicated to serving others.

One of my best friends growing up was Kyle Kingsbury, who stepped up on my behalf when I was in the eighth grade at a new school. He stood up to the bullies who picked on me for wearing shorter shorts than them and being in special education classes. His support was a turning point for me—it meant the world to have someone like him in a new school stand up for me. Our friendship grew, and I remember arm wrestling him one day; I was the only one in the school who could beat him. I believe he respected me for having so much strength. The things that can spark a friendship in kids, huh?

Kyle later became a professional mixed martial artist, the only other one from Cupertino, California, besides myself. Watching him get over his own challenges and succeed as both a fighter and an entrepreneur has continually inspired me to strive for greatness in my own life. Since retiring from fighting, Kyle has built a farm in Texas with his family. He has not only cultivated an amazing life, but now trains, encourages, and coaches others around the world to do the same. I'm really proud of who he has become as a man and father, and I'm blessed he is one of my friends to this day.

Another significant influence has been Tammy Pugh, who is now a Superintendent at Foundation Academies. The section below was written by her, and exemplifies how we formed a bond based on selfless significance:

For over twelve years, I have had the privilege of working alongside Daniel, a journey that began before he had even established his first school. We were introduced by my head of security Brian, back when I was a school principal in Buffalo, NY. Brian essentially said, "I know you are in California this week and you HAVE to meet this guy." Daniel's nonprofit was just getting going around this time, so really he was just looking for an opportunity to spread his message and put his ideas into action. We were provided this opportunity for Daniel to come in and mentor our students and teachers across four different schools since this chance meeting. We took this opportunity and Daniel made a genuine impact on many of the staff and students that he came across. Daniel also did this for almost no financial gain, since there was not a lot to spend on building emotional intelligence and your belief systems back then. This was all about spreading his program and seeing how it could and would work. Now that's what I call selfless significance. Daniel has exemplified that since day one.

Daniel was and is determined to make a difference in the

lives of kids who were often overlooked or faced overwhelming odds. Driven by a vision of inspiring and empowering young adults who might not have another chance, Daniel committed himself wholeheartedly to this new work. His unwavering dedication and approach brought life to our classrooms, and it even extended to my home life. My youngest son, Kai, was mentored by Daniel through his White Belt program, which Kai himself would go on to assist with later on. He and Mason, my older son, traveled with Daniel to India on multiple occasions in order to help at-risk youth and meet with high-ranking educators. It is as if his relentless pursuit of significance creates a sort of gravitational pull, which makes people he interacts with become better versions of themselves.

Over the years, Daniel's hard work and dedication has allowed him to expand his reach from a single school to a multi-state network that now spans three states. This growth wasn't the result of quick success, but of years of inspiring children, training educators, and investing in communities one by one. I've watched as Daniel built a foundation grounded in belief systems, vision, and commitment.

Now, I am honored to work alongside him as we continue this journey together. With a presence across three states, we have the opportunity to support thousands of students, empowering them to overcome obstacles, embrace their goals, and go beyond even their own expectations. I have always chased the greatest impact when it comes to education, which I think is a big reason why Daniel and I have been able to work together so effectively for this long. It is deeply fulfilling to witness how his early vision has evolved into a mission of lasting impact that will continue to touch lives far into the future.

These experiences have shaped not only my career but also my understanding of what it means to live a life of significance. Both Kai and Tammy have taught me that real fulfillment comes not from material success but from the impact we have on others' lives. Their stories remind me that in any field, including law enforcement and education, the opportunity to serve and uplift others is a path to personal growth and satisfaction. My only hope is that I've positively influenced them half as much as they have me!

Puder's Journal about Selfless Significance

Think about the most significant thing you do in your life right now. That which impacts the most people in a positive way. Do you believe you do it selflessly, or do you do it, at least in part, because you expect something in return?

Write your thoughts here:

_____

_____

_____

_____

_____

_____

_____

How can you change your mindset in order to be selfless in your pursuit of significance?

_____

_____

_____

_____

_____

_____

_____

Chapter 5: No Job Too Small

You often hear the story of the CEO of a Fortune 500 company having worked a low-level menial label job in his or her youth. "So-and-so is one of the richest people in the world, but he was once a janitor," the headline will read. Is it a coincidence that so many of the most successful people on Earth were not simply handed the keys to their kingdom, but started in entry level jobs? **It's not.**

Because in life, no job should be too small. No job should be beneath you. And every job gives you the opportunity to be significant in some way.

Daniel Puder: Bathroom Cleaner

The first job I ever had was cleaning toilets as a 12-year-old. Yep, you read that right. My dad owned a business called UVEXS Inc, which handles UV ink printing and equipment, and decided to put my free labor to good use; working to maintain the cleanliness of his facilities, which would teach me a skillset. You can imagine what a 12-year-old Daniel Puder thought when he found out this is what he'd be doing for his first internship. This isn't fun. This isn't fair. My dad is being a jerk. The usual things adolescents think when they're put to work. The lessons

I learned from this experience would be extremely significant, however, as you'll soon see. I was blessed to have my father who spent quality time teaching me the fundamentals of hard work within his company.

Cleaning toilets taught me that, for a business to function properly, every employee needs to be contributing to the best of his or her abilities. From the CEO all the way down to, well, me, wiping down porcelain. If even one person is not fulfilling certain duties, it sends a ripple all the way up and through the chain of command, one that each employee around them is affected by. If the bathrooms weren't clean, this worsened the experience of customers whenever they used the facilities, or employees when they needed a break. If the mindset of the customers and/or employees was impacted, this would show in the overall performance of the business.

From my current viewpoint, embracing a "get to" rather than a "have to" mentality can transform an organization's culture and environment. I aim to motivate individuals to excel daily. It doesn't matter if they remain in our organization or eventually move to another—or even start their own. Witnessing people chase their dreams with the same energy I have, investing their time, talent, and resources to build something of their own, is truly exhilarating.

I remember watching and listening to Gary Vaynerchuk, commonly known as Gary Vee, in a video where an interesting exchange took place. After watching Gary warmly embrace someone when he got out of an elevator, the person who was meeting him asked if the person was a family member or friend. Gary's response highlighted his philosophy. "No, that's one of our team members; we're building a family here." This idea is central to his leadership style; everyone is on the same team and working towards the same goal. Equals. In another segment of his show, Gary spoke about his willingness to support team members seeking new opportunities elsewhere. However, he also made it clear that returning to the team after leaving for slightly better pay elsewhere wouldn't be an option. If you're just looking for more money over a better culture, that's not an employee who aligns with his vision.

This philosophy of every member of a company being part of a big team speaks to some of my own experiences, particularly during my early days cleaning bathrooms. While many might dismiss this type of work as beneath them, it was invaluable to me. This role was part of my father's business and taught me not only the importance of maintaining a sanitary environment but also the dignity in all types of work. It was more than just a job; it gave me an opportunity to appreciate those in cleaning and janitorial roles and to understand that no job should be looked down upon.

From 12 to 19 years old, my dad put me to work with all of his different managers, all of whom taught me how to work in their departments. I look back on this period as being a really cool time in my life because most people don't get to go to work with their fathers. I've taken a similar approach with my son, even though he's only three. He's not quite ready to work for Foundation Academies, but the concept of working with me has been reinforced since he was old enough to follow directions. I remember one day when he was about two, there was a vacuum cleaner in a room in our house. He said, Papa, I want to do that. I said, sure. So we vacuumed the room together, and we continue to accomplish these types of tasks whenever we can.

Real life can be so much fun, but most people look down on the routine things that happen on a daily basis, mostly related to their jobs. They don't enjoy them, which would be solved by a "get-to" attitude, as opposed to a "have-to" attitude. These little things every single day can make a big impact in people's lives. Every time our head company cleaner, Miss D, cleans our facility, it is spotless to the highest level. She does it all with a smile and without a complaint. This is someone with a get-to attitude.

My experience in these roles in my dad's company gave me some practical skills that will always be valuable. It also allowed me to relate to workers in positions often overlooked by society. This early job laid the groundwork for many of our company's Standard Operating Procedures (SOPs), when we later established a janitorial service for our private schools. Having firsthand knowledge of the work involved made it easier to identify and explain what was required, improving our hiring process and efficiency.

This hands-on background was also crucial in one particular instance recently when we needed to replace one of our cleaning consultants. We finally found the right person this year, who has significantly improved the cleanliness of our campuses and headquarters. Recognizing her contributions, I recently gave her a $200 Amazon gift card as a token of appreciation. Gestures like this one, though small, can have a major impact, offering the person the chance to either enjoy or share the gift with someone they care about.

Whether it's leading an organization or performing tasks some people consider lowly, the concepts of respect, empathy, and commitment are the same. By creating a supportive and inclusive environment and recognizing the significance of every role, we create a path for both personal and organizational success. This approach not only enhances our operations but also our community, making each day an opportunity to "get to" make a difference rather than just "having to" do a job.

Early Businesses and Careers

At the age of 17, I ventured into the world of painting. This was basically the start of my entrepreneurial journey. My first project was for my wrestling coach, Dave, who needed someone to paint the exterior of his house. Confidently, I assured him I could handle the job. Although my only exposure to painting was watching a friend of mine do some jobs, I was eager to try my hand at it. In 2000, I completed that paint job for Dave's house, and remarkably, when I visited the house again in 2023, the paint still looked fresh after 23 years.

This success inspired me to look for more painting opportunities. I began to connect with other clients within my network, painting homes and buildings and gradually building a reputation in the community. My enthusiasm for the work grew and I invested in a $5,000 sprayer, which allowed me to complete projects quicker. This tool not only improved my productivity but also enhanced the quality of my work. I took on more jobs and expanded my client base.

At 19, my entrepreneurial spirit led me to start a screen printing and banner printing business. I bought a four-press screen printing shirt machine and a 60-inch banner machine, which could operate simultaneously with the shirt printing. This setup was ideal because the banner machine was automatic, allowing me to maximize my productivity by doing multiple tasks at once. This dual operation proved to be a good strategy; it gave me two streams of income from the same investment. I ran this business from the ages of 19 to 21, until I transitioned into a career in the WWE.

During my time in the WWE, my focus shifted away from my businesses back home in order to concentrate on my athletic career. However, the skills and experiences I gained from running those small businesses played a significant role in my approach to my career. Each job I've had has taught me valuable lessons about service, work ethic, and the importance of being significant in whatever task I'm performing.

These early experiences laid a solid foundation for my role as a business owner at the helm of Foundation Academies today. The hands-on skills and the ability to juggle multiple projects not only prepared me for the many tasks of running an educational organization, but also taught me the value of hard work and self-reliance.

Reflecting on these early years, I recognize how starting small, getting my hands dirty, and embracing every opportunity to learn and grow were crucial to my development. These jobs were not just about making money; they were about creating value and making a positive impact on those around me. The discipline and determination I learned from balancing painting, screen printing, and eventually a professional wrestling career helped me build the resilience and leadership qualities necessary for success in any field. Today, as I look back at my journey from a young painter to an entrepreneur and professional athlete, I appreciate how each phase of my life contributed to my understanding of business and service. The idea of "significance breeds success" continues to influence how I lead and inspire others, showing that with the right attitude and work ethic, you can turn any skill or opportunity into a launching pad for bigger and better achievements.

American Kickboxing Academy

Let me take you back to this time, but from a sports perspective. I am in high school, am a pretty solid wrestler, and I am looking for something more in the world of mixed martial arts. I decided to shoot for the stars: the famous American Kickboxing Academy, or simply AKA, of San Jose, California. At 17 years old I walked into American Kickboxing Academy, the home of multiple-time kickboxing world champion Javier Mendez, looking to train. He gave me a one-week pass for free.

AKA is one of the biggest names in combat sports, specifically mixed martial arts, boxing and kickboxing. Some of the sport's greatest champions have trained there. I'm talking about guys like Cain Velazquez, Daniel Cormier, Khabib Nurmagomedov, Islam Makhachev, and more. They have all come through AKA at one point. I decided that, if I wanted to make it as a fighter, this was where I needed to hone my craft. There was only one tiny problem. I didn't have the money to pay for a membership. It was not cheap.

When I first stepped into the American Kickboxing Academy, I signed up for MMA training with Frank Shamrock, who is a 5x UFC champion and trainer. Starting day one, I jumped in the class and started training with some of the top fighters in the world. They mix the pro fighters with non-pros when doing MMA training, which gives them different perspectives on how to train and who to train with, depending on their size, strength, and other attributes. Frank Shamrock was the lead trainer for every one of these night classes. My buddy Kyle Kingsbury, who you learned about last chapter, and I would go to these training sessions and relish in the competition.

Training in mixed martial arts at a professional gym like this was much different than the typical workout at a regular gym. Here, if trainers saw potential in you, they'd pair you with the tough guys or the professional athletes. These top fighters would really test my mental toughness with their skill sets and physical ability. Despite the physical challenges, I found myself thriving. There was something about the strategy, the rigorous exercise, and the release of pent-up energy I couldn't get enough of. By the end of the week, even though I was far from matching the skill levels of these experienced fighters, I still wanted more.

Most people go to a gym to do cardio, lift weights, or maybe take a class like yoga or pilates for a week or two on a free trial. But in an MMA gym, they just kick your ass for that week instead. Some people stay, but most will leave. It's interesting to see people's reactions when they get pushed to a certain level. There will be those who want more and are willing to push themselves harder, learn, and take a whooping. Then there are those who leave after day one because their ego is so fragile that they can't take not being right or winning all the time. I find this is true in all aspects of life. If you want to test yourself, go to an MMA gym. See how you respond to a new and unfamiliar setting. Can you handle it?

A new challenge presented itself when the free week ended: the cost of continuing. The membership fee was $150 a month. Like any normal kid would do, I went to my parents and asked them for the money. Unfortunately for me, a few months before I took my free trial at AKA, I was sent to juvenile hall for fighting. My parents' response was that they had just paid my legal fees to get me out of trouble, and that they didn't want to fund me learning how to be even more dangerous as a fighter. As a parent myself, this makes complete sense to me today, but back then, I really wanted them to support my passion. It was more about the physicality and energy of the sport that attracted me to it than the actual fighting.

I was now faced with this financial hurdle, but I

knew I had to find a way to train at the American Kickboxing Academy. I started thinking, what else could I do to be able to get a membership? What value could I provide, other than a membership fee? Then it hit me: why not use a skill I had developed while working for my dad's company? Cleaning.

I had become pretty good at cleaning bathrooms, thanks to my past job. I told Javier I could take over the cleaning responsibilities at the gym in exchange for my membership, and he said yes. This was my official start at the American Kickboxing Academy. It wasn't as a fighter in the ring, but as the one who cleaned the facilities. I maintained the gym's bathrooms and mats each week, a task I continued until a newer member took over the responsibility, allowing me to finally focus solely on training.

This experience taught me valuable lessons about determination, resourcefulness, and the importance of seizing opportunities. By trading my skills for training, I not only managed to pursue my passion for mixed martial arts but also learned the significance of work ethic and humility. Each day spent cleaning was a reminder of what it takes to achieve your goals, no matter the arena. This period of my life was a big part of the foundation for the fighter and human I would become.

Looking back at where I was, Javier Mendez gave me an opportunity that probably saved my life. I was young and angry, and didn't understand what was going on deep in my heart and mind. Javier has done this for so many athletes; you would be blown away by the impact he has made in this world. The significance of one man can not be overstated and there's no telling how much good a person can do. Our methods of being significant are obviously different, but my goal in life is to be as significant as somebody like Javier Mendez. To this day he continues to impact the world through his gym, his love and care for others, and his wisdom. It's been a blessing to stay in contact with him over the years and see his growth within the mixed martial arts space. I'm blessed to have this man in my life and I'm excited to see what comes next.

Now, back to Frank Shamrock. There are probably a lot

of fighters who have also cleaned toilets or done some sort of entry level job at some point, but there are very few who got to train with Frank Shamrock at the highest level. Frank is one-of-a-kind as a trainer, coach, and friend. Frank took me under his wing while he was training, such as in the leadup to his Tito Ortiz fight. I remember riding in a van with Frank and a few other fighters to a fight in the middle of nowhere in California one day. Frank was driving the van and we laughed and joked the whole time there and back.

Frank is creative, intelligent, and a really hard worker in and outside the ring. Being a five-time UFC champion is not an easy task; the things I saw Frank do in order to compete and beat the best of the best were incredible. To gain weight, he would wake up in the middle of night and have an extra meal. At the gym he would go longer and harder than any other fighter, coming in first and leaving last. He also knew exactly how to dial in his cardio routine to cut weight, which he taught me. This helped me tremendously as a fighter.

A lot of people in life look for the coach who is the biggest or strongest, but I think there's a lot more to be said for the wisdom that coaches provide, which cannot be measured by looking at them. Frank taught me it wasn't about the submission but it was about the position before the submission. He was a very intelligent fighter who created strategy not just using his body, but his brain as well. He understood his opponent better than they did sometimes. This is how he was able to capitalize on so many of their weaknesses and become a champion, even when he wasn't the strongest man in the cage. I'm blessed I had Frank in my life and as my first MMA coach for the foundation and support he gave me.

It got to the point while training at AKA that some people would call me Junior, because Frank and I were so close. I wasn't the best athlete in the world, but one thing I did was work really hard. I wasn't the best fighter or wrestler either, but I pushed myself past the point that most people would quit. I learned how to learn, how to grow, and how to evolve my body, mind, and spirit to become a more formidable mixed martial artist. I'm sure there are plenty of other aspiring fighters out there trying to scrape by while cleaning bathrooms in order to pay for a membership, like I did. Unfortunately, many of them will give up before they reach their full potential, be it due to not having good mentors to push them, or just not having the right mentality to chase a vision with everything they have to give.

I challenge you to accomplish two things. Number one, I challenge you to find the best coach you can. Someone like Frank who practices what he preaches and treats you like his equal. A person you aspire to be. Number two, be brave, build grit, and love what you do every day, because when those punches and kicks come, literally or figuratively, and you're hurting physically, emotionally, or spiritually, you will remain standing. Your mentality and the ones you've surrounded yourself with have given you the boost you need to never surrender.

That is what Frank and Javier taught me through their words and their actions, both in and out of the gym.

Significance Everywhere

Every job, from the top to the bottom of the Totem Pole, gave me the opportunity to be significant for someone else. This mentality that was instilled in me early on has helped me as a business owner. At Foundation Academies, executives all the way down to our newest hires for entry-level positions all get to do things that are not necessarily our job. We also get to teach people how to do those things because managers need to understand how the little things work so the organization can grow.

My goal with my team is to be able to support their growth and give them the right mentorship so the company can become the most significant school system in the world. There are so many companies that are more focused on money and success than the people running the operation. I'm not saying our way is perfect, because there's a strategy and purpose to both sides. But our company was built on being significant and building a culture where everyone thrives. So far, it's worked out better than I could have imagined.

Each person in our company has the ability to be significant in some way towards our students, parents, and the communities we exist in. They also have the potential to teach me something about life, significance, a way of thinking, behaving, or even a new skill. To put it simply, my growth is caused by the people around me.

If my personal situation is any indication, you never know when you're in the process of acquiring a skill that will benefit you in some way down the road. What if I would've been stubborn and not helped my dad with his business's bathroom?

Would I have found another way to join the American Kickboxing Academy? Maybe, but maybe not. Cleaning bathrooms for my dad, no matter how much I disliked it at the time, led to much of my success as a professional fighter and who I have become today. You could make the argument it helped me even more as a fighter than as an entrepreneur, because the repercussions for not learning quickly and correctly are you getting seriously injured. If you fail as a CEO, you simply go out of business and try again. I had to learn these skills fast as a teenager. They made me significant.

You have already seen examples in this book of how significance breeds success, and you will learn of many more. But this story right here might be the clearest one I've ever experienced. **There's no job too small for a person chasing significance!**

Significance in the WWE

When I first appeared on WWE Smackdown, I found myself with time to spare before my event. Instead of sitting idly, I approached the ring setup team and offered to help them build the ring. There were several wrestlers around, just waiting for the setup to be completed so they could start their pre-show training. But instead of joining them in waiting, I decided to be proactive and learn a new skill, while helping accelerate the process for everyone.

Interestingly, this little gesture had a ripple effect. After I started helping with the ring, Al Snow, a well-known wrestler I mentioned earlier, insisted that all WWE Tough Enough contestants participate in setting up the ring every week. While I thought the process was pretty enjoyable and a great opportunity to make new friends and learn a skill, some of the other contestants saw it differently. They saw it as beneath them, just a tedious chore. They were focused solely on becoming wrestlers, missing the broader picture of what it takes to thrive in the industry.

These small acts of stepping up continued throughout the eight-week competition on Smackdown, during which I not only gained physical skills but also built valuable relationships. I connected with the videographers, audio team, writers, and even staff back in headquarters in Connecticut. One of them told me when I came back to town after Smackdown taping that I was going to win. I looked at him and said thank you so much, only thinking he was a fan and not understanding who he was. After I won Tough Enough and became the champion, I went back to headquarters to get some work done and meet with some of their teams. Funny enough, I saw the same guy smoking a cigarette around the same place in the parking lot as the first time. He looked at me and said, "I told you you would win." I asked him how he knew. He said he was in charge of the fan vote and he saw the trends of how I was performing. When I wrestled Kurt Angle I got a huge bump in the polls and fan votes. He said he was a fan and I did great. These interactions put an important lesson on display; you never know who you'll meet or where those connections will lead in life.

I challenge anybody to be ready for the opportunity when it comes. I challenge people to be organized, focused, and driven, all in preparation for the right moment. Search for the things you want, don't just wait for them to fall on your lap, because that day may never come. Like people seek out food when they are hungry, you can search for the right people and opportunities through preparation and work ethic. For me as a business owner this means that if I want to get a loan, my accounting documents are all in order and ready to be submitted. When I want to speak on stage, I have my speech organized, a highlight video ready, and I've rehearsed it until it is perfect. Be ready for the opportunity, because people can't be significant towards you if you're not ready to accept their influence.

During the eight-week WWE Tough Enough Championship I stayed in Stamford, Connecticut for the whole duration. I then traveled when I had to go on the road for the tapings of Smackdown. All the other seven contestants returned home to go party with their friends and family. I'm not knocking what they did, but for me, when I'm focused on something, I want to put 100% effort into achieving my goals. My coaches told me if you focus on one thing, you can do it really well and achieve the results you're looking for. Staying in Stamford also meant less travel, giving me a bit more downtime, although I packed those moments with activities to maximize every opportunity.

I spent several hours daily on various aspects of my career beyond physical training. This included working on promos, focusing on marketing and branding, developing a website, and strategizing with my mentors, including Dave Meltzer, the founder of the Wrestling Observer Newsletter. This preparation was crucial, as the competition was partly decided by fan votes. By throwing myself into all aspects of the business, I tried to leave no stone unturned in my quest to come out on top.

This was an intense period of my life. It was when I learned the value of embracing every task, no matter how small it might seem. Whether it was setting up a ring or strategizing promotional efforts, I realized that every action could contribute to larger success. The mindset of seeing no job as too small or insignificant helped me not only in the competition but has continued to influence how I approach my career and life.

Ultimately, this approach helped me win the Million

Dollar Tough Enough challenge on Smackdown. It wasn't just about the physical training or the performances in the ring; it was also about the relationships built, the skills learned, and the overall approach to my career. This experience reinforced that in life and careers, success often comes from a willingness to fully commit, learn from every good or bad situation, and value every contribution, no matter how small it seems.

Remember to value every person and every moment. Whether it's a brief conversation with someone in a seemingly minor role or taking the time to enhance your well-being, each aspect plays a part in shaping your path to success. No effort is too small when it comes to building a meaningful, healthy life and achieving lasting significance.

Puder's Journal About No Job Too Small

Here's my challenge for you. This week, I want you to do something you consider a small task. Something you'd probably never do, as you'd usually let someone else take care of it. Maybe you think you're above this sort of thing, or that you just don't have to do it because it's someone else's job. Or maybe it is your job and you just won't do it unless you have to. Well this week, you do it with a get-to attitude and you do your best to enjoy it. Recount the experience below:

What "small" job or action did you partake in?

_____

_____

_____

_____

_____

_____

How did it make you feel?

_____

_____

_____

_____

_____

_____

If it's a negative feeling, write here where you think this feeling comes from. Process if this feeling serves you, and if it doesn't, choose a different way.

_____

_____

_____

_____

_____

_____

Chapter 6: Spiritual Significance

Significance takes on a much more powerful meaning when there's an element of spirituality thrown into it. I'm not going to sit here and push a certain religion or belief system on you. I'm here to tell you how it affected me personally, as someone constantly striving for significance.

I was raised in a Christian family in a house where both parents were very supportive. We went to a youth group on Wednesday nights and church on the weekends. I built a unique and beautiful relationship with God when I was young. As I grew up, I started to understand how to connect with the Holy Spirit further. I believe some of the challenges I have been through mentally, emotionally, physically, and definitely spiritually improved my ability to listen and keep myself open to God's grace. One of my philosophies in life is to do as it says in the Bible; never stop praying. I believe there's a big difference between connecting our higher self to the Holy Spirit and simply praying at breakfast, lunch, and dinner.

I got to meet His Holiness the Dalai Lama in 2018. A lot of my friends who are Christian thought I might not be able to connect with him due to him practicing a different religion in Buddhism. When I was with him and listening to him, however, I saw that, although we worship different Gods, his main goal in life was also to lift his spirit and the spirits of others. He has created joy, passion, peace, and love for so many people through his words and actions. I got to witness other young Buddhists who followed him spend hours every day strengthening their mind, building up their endurance of meditation, which is their form of prayer.

They also took good care of their bodies through a good diet and exercise regimen. I believe more people, whether Christians or followers of any other religion, need to see the dedication that these young Buddhist monks use to become the best version of themselves. These are things that translate to any person, regardless of which holy book you believe in, if any. For me though, the Bible was my source of spirituality, and I've used its teachings to inspire my behavior as a husband, father, business owner, and yes, even as a fighter.

My Spirituality

Fighters all have their own routines before and after fights. A major aspect of my routine was to pray before and after I did my thing in the ring. I did this for two reasons. The first one was to show people what's possible when you have connection with God and you dedicate your life to serving His purpose on Earth. The second one was for me to give him thanks for all his blessings. I'd get on a knee in the middle of the cage, what did I care about what people thought? I wanted to show how thankful I was for all the gifts bestowed upon me, and ask to keep me safe as I put my body on the line. Once the fight was over, I wanted to thank the Lord that I was in one piece, while also asking Him to keep my opponent healthy in the aftermath of our battle.

Faith has been a major catalyst behind much of my efforts as a fighter and entrepreneur. I've found that, when you don't just believe in a higher power, but use that power from the Holy Spirit in order to better yourself, the challenges in your professional and personal life become easier to manage and overcome.

Throughout my life, I've had moments where I could sense events before they happened, or feel a deep connection to decisions and life choices. Whether it's a finely-tuned sense of energy or something, I'm not sure. But these experiences have often guided me, improving my understanding and approach to life's challenges.

Growing up, I was always very intuitive. I felt a strong understanding of how things worked around me. However, during my teenage years, I found myself drifting away from this spiritual connection. It wasn't until I entered the worlds of professional fighting and wrestling that I saw lifestyles and behaviors that I didn't want to emulate, which in turn increased my relationship with God and took my spiritual connection to the next level.

This focus has greatly impacted how I view challenges and interact with others today. I often think about whether people are living in line with what I consider their higher self—kind of like the Holy Spirit—or whether they are driven by their ego. As a professional athlete, I had a mixture of ego-driven desires, like chasing fame, attention, and wealth. I always had a sense of giving back, thankfully, as I was also supporting local youth programs, hospitals, and other groups. Over time, I've come to realize even more the importance of living a life that is filled with deeper values and a higher spiritual calling.

Nowadays, I look at life through a lens formed by these spiritual experiences. I believe being connected to the Holy Spirit, or one's higher self, can and does influence how we live and interact with the world. It's not just about achieving personal success or building wealth; it's about fulfilling a deeper purpose and making meaningful connections. I think every person has a spirit that was put in a body on Earth in order to be the representation of God in their own way.

My spiritual journey has taught me the value of nurturing your soul. It is natural for a person to shoot for success, but the significant part comes from doing so in a way that is aligned with his or her beliefs and values. In the end, these experiences have reinforced my faith and continued to shape how I look at the world and my place in it.

Generational Challenges

I recently watched a movie called All the Money in the World, which delves into the dramatic saga of the Getty family. In the film, one of the younger Gettys is kidnapped, and his grandfather, the billionaire J. Paul Getty, who amassed a fortune in the oil industry, refuses to pay the ransom. This leads to a big exchange with one of his aides in charge of recovering the grandson. When the aide questions what it would take to secure the boy's release, Getty replies that he doesn't have the finances and requires more money to handle the situation, even though this isn't true. This scenario illuminates a profound truth about wealth: no matter how much we have, we can't take it with us when we die.

Many people work and work and work to build massive companies, often becoming the first in their families to have such extreme wealth. They pass these businesses on to their children, hoping to set up lasting legacies. However, statistically, these fortunes tend to disappear within three to four generations. I think there are several reasons for this trend. Firstly, the vision and culture of the company, as established by its founder, affects how future generations perceive and manage the wealth and the business. If the original vision isn't clearly communicated or maintained, the business can lose its way.

I believe the most important reason, though, is that it takes a certain level of grit, wisdom, and spiritual strength to get through the tough times and build or maintain something. It is generally not as respected when someone is given something in life, as opposed to when the person earns it. For the generation that is handed the keys once the founder passes away or steps down, they usually don't have the skills their predecessor developed through overcoming challenges.

This has been one of my thoughts for my son Konrad. How do I add value to his life by buying the right amount of things he can use to learn and grow? How do I love him the right amount so that he knows I love him and connect with him, while also helping him love himself? How do I push him to be passionate about life, and build the grit and wisdom it takes to impact the world?

Son, you're three and a half years old when I'm writing this book. When you read this someday, when you hopefully understand how important you are to me, how much time I spend on you and how much I love you, I hope you remember this and pass it on to the next generation.

Many sons and daughters of business owners may not have a deep knowledge of the business like their parents did. They also don't have the spiritual fortitude needed to grow the company past the levels of those who came before them. The drive and resilience required to build a multi million or multi billion-dollar company from scratch often comes from personal challenges or motivations these children have not experienced. Not everyone has the spirit to sacrifice their nights, weekends, and personal life, or work 80 to 100 hours a week, to grow a business.

This is a critical lesson about wealth and legacy. While financial success gives you many opportunities, it does not guarantee happiness or fulfillment, not like an elevated spirit does. It also shows the importance of fostering strong family bonds with solid values, and preparing the next generation not just to inherit wealth, but to build upon it with purpose, passion, and perseverance. As we go down our own paths, whether in business or personal life, it's important to remember that the true value of our effort is not just wealth, but the legacy we leave behind.

Spiritual Leaders

About 16 years ago, my life took an important turn when I relocated to Los Angeles and met Harlan Gittin, a man who would become a mentor and like a second father to me. Harlan was not only a successful businessman in the automobile industry, owning multiple dealerships that sold brands like Toyota and BMW, but he was also deeply committed to his family, always prioritizing them above his professional achievements. His guidance opened my eyes to the power of balancing personal and professional life.

Harlan introduced me to some of the wealthiest people in the world, giving me insights and advice during my late twenties. These experiences under his mentorship helped shape my understanding of success, not just as a measure of wealth, but as a reflection of a person's values and priorities. This view of success resonated with me, influencing the way I approached life and business.

During this period, I also explored the relationship between chasing success to satisfy my ego and aligning my actions with my "higher self." It was clear that many people chase fulfillment and connection through external validation, like a big house or fast cars. They don't pay as much attention to the internal journey that leads to true satisfaction and purpose. This led to me analyzing how I could use a more purposeful and introspective approach in my life.

As I said earlier, a particularly enlightening experience occurred when I traveled to India to attend an event by His Holiness the Dalai Lama, right before Black Friday. The Dalai Lama shared an impactful story about people in India who traveled for days, some walking for four to five days, to attend his event, which drew a crowd of over 100,000. This was a huge contrast to the consumer-driven frenzy typical of Black Friday in the United States, where people camp outside stores to snag the latest products when the doors open. These people in India were on a real quest. They were there to grow spiritually, mentally, physically, and emotionally by absorbing wisdom from the Dalai Lama.

The difference between the materialistic pursuits in the West and the spiritual journeys in other parts of the world was eye-opening. At the event, despite the poverty of much of the attendees—the children played barefoot on the dirt, clearly owning very little—they showed a level of joy that seemed to be higher than that of many wealthier families in more developed countries. The people took care of us extremely well, supporting our trip when we were out there and feeding us with delicious Indian specialties. I am so blessed to have experienced this trip. This observation showed me the huge difference in life perspectives and what truly causes happiness and fulfillment.

These experiences have affected my opinion of spiritual connection and purpose. My goals center around my family, our company, our staff, and the service we provide to the community, particularly through our schools and nonprofit work. Yet, defining my purpose can be simplified to core principles that guide my daily actions and decisions. It is encapsulated in one word: Love. This includes different forms of love—tough love, gentle love, and educational love—all of which are meant to nurture and support those around me.

While some may challenge the idea of tough love, saying that it can be overly harsh, I believe there are moments in life when you need a firm approach. This should always be rooted in genuine concern and care, coming from a perspective that encourages growth, even if it may be uncomfortable at first.

My journey through mentorship, spiritual exploration, and personal and professional challenges has taught me the importance of looking beyond achievements to find true success. It's about nurturing genuine connections, staying true to your values, and always striving to be the best version of oneself. The quest for a meaningful, fulfilled life is a continuous journey that shapes our worldview and actions. It reminds us that no job is too small and no act of kindness is insignificant in the pursuit of a spiritual life well-lived.

Love and Fear

Over the past ten to twelve years, my life has been shaped by a growing sense of intentionality. At some point in every day, I dedicate some time to what some might call meditation or prayer. I'm just keeping my ears open and hearing what the Holy Spirit wants to teach me. This practice is based on the belief that spiritual engagement is important. My goal is to maintain a constant connection with the Holy Spirit, and this means I have to nurture this relationship daily.

This journey of deep spiritual engagement has also taught me the difference between love and fear, two powerful forces in their own right. An important conversation with a man I call a friend, someone I first knew as Coach Joe, shows this concept.

The first conversation I ever had with Joe was at a small event in South Florida. The group was reading a book called The Course in Miracles. There's a part of the book that reads, "The opposite of love is fear, but what is all-encompassing can have no opposite." When we think using love, we are literally co-creating with God. And when we're not thinking with love, since only love is real, then we're actually not thinking at all.
I have to be honest, I didn't really think that statement was true before I met Coach Joe. I was specifically skeptical of the part related to fear. Coach Joe and I got into a friendly debate about it, and he asked me why I thought it wasn't true. I said I thought fear is not real. He asks why not. I said because we as humans have an immaterial ego, and that is responsible for making up fear. Although he disagreed, he appreciated my unique thoughts on the matter. This was the start of a long friendship.

Coach Joe is very good at understanding how different people communicate, how they think, and how to help them create the results they're looking for. Joe asked me where do fears come from? What causes the ego to create them? I thought to myself for a minute, before finally replying that I didn't know. He said all fears come from loss. Humans and our egos don't want loss. Fears are fundamentally framed to protect us from things that could potentially come with loss, be it physical, mental, or spiritual.

I thought about this for a while. When you Google "fear", one of the top results that come up is public speaking. Public speaking is not really the fear though, is it? It's fear of the unknown. It's fear of what might or might not happen. When you're publicly speaking, people might say things about you.

When you're building a company, you might fail. Figuring out your greatest fears can be a valuable tool, for now you know what is holding you back. I believe giving in to fear in life will make you sick, angry, and hurt. When you feel off and not aligned with your inner essence, there may be some type of crippling fear somewhere in your life that needs to be addressed.

Love is powerful. I believe God is, essentially, love, and love creates peace in our lives. It frees us from the bondage of fear and all that fear can bring to our lives. Love gives you the motivation to get up in the morning and bring joy to the world. I believe every single person on this Earth was put here to represent God's voice, image, or expression on this Earth.

The conversations I had with Coach Joe that night were some of the most impactful conversations I've ever had in my life. It helped show me how to make better decisions and analyze the things standing in the way of me achieving my vision.

Love, for me, is greater than any emotion; it is an active force that drives passion, creates peace, encourages bravery, and instills resilience. Choosing to be guided by the spiritual significance of love has been a blessing. It's made me a better person in every way possible.

In the broader scope of life, understanding and embracing spirituality can vary among different people. Some may not believe in a spiritual realm or have a relationship with a "higher power," sometimes because they need physical proof or logical justification for this type of thing. However, I challenge everyone to explore their own spirituality through thought and meditation, not just for a short period, but as a continuous, deep journey of self-discovery. Analyzing your own spiritual being, which we all have, means looking inward to discover the best version of oneself.

Engaging with your spiritual self doesn't really align with any one religion. It just involves connecting with the highest part of your being. The inner self is what I consider the peak of personal significance. By connecting with this part of you, you not only enrich your personal life, but also improve your capacity to impact the world around you.

Spiritual development never stops and is filled with challenges. It requires us to be introspective, patient, and open to changing how we look at ourselves and our interactions with the world. For me, embracing spirituality has meant living a life filled with love. I can always talk about rejecting fear, or tell myself that I won't be affected by whatever stands in my way. The problem is this is the same concept as the school programs that went around and told kids don't do drugs or bully others. They don't work and there are now studies showing that focusing on what should be done, as opposed to what shouldn't be done, is far more effective. You and I are both powerful. What we focus on, if we do it with the right intention and commitment, we will achieve. **Let's focus on our spiritual well-being a bit more.**

Puder's Journal on Spiritual Significance

If you are comfortable with spirituality of some kind, write down what your vision is for where you want to be spiritually. Your inside. Your core. How do you want that being to uplift you and how will you improve your life through your higher self?

_____

_____

_____

_____

_____

_____

_____

_____

_____

_____

_____

_____

Once you've written down a few things here, think about how you can commit maybe 1% of your time focusing on yourself. I used to use cardio, working out, a cold plunge, or the beach to be able to spend quality time by myself, just to connect with my thoughts and emotions. 1% of your time is 1.68 hours per week, which I'm sure you can afford. This focusing time will help you self-reflect and analyze where you stand, and how you can change things for the better.

_____

_____

_____

_____

_____

_____

_____

_____

_____

_____

Chapter 7: Significant Moments

The most significant moments are not always recognizable as they happen. It's only in looking back that we see their true impact. Throughout my life, many people have blessed me with the significance of their actions and words. It takes a village to achieve anything noteworthy, as they say.

The notion of being "self-made" is, in my opinion, impossible. No one achieves greatness by themselves. Those who concentrate on creating significance naturally attract like-minded individuals. This process is what creates meaningful connections between people who are out to change the world for the better.

One man in particular, named David Homan, is a perfect example of this concept. The following is an excerpt that covers a little about how I met this extraordinary individual, and what significance means to him:

In the intriguing realm of professional connections and purposeful networking, I, David Homan, found a kindred spirit in Daniel Puder. Though a classical composer by trade, I established Orchestrated Connecting LLC just over eight years ago. Orchestrated Connecting as an entrepreneurial networking venture designed to bring together proactive and generous individuals through social gatherings. This initiative strives for what I term "purposeful connectivity and community," a process that draws individuals from incredibly diverse backgrounds; the majority of our network is women and/or people of color from an impressive span of 167 cities across 34 countries. These individuals share a common ethos of curiosity and a desire to construct systemic solutions for global betterment.

Daniel Puder was among the early supporters of Orchestrated Connecting, embodying the very ideals the organization champions. At Orchestrated Connecting, there is no elitism or hierarchical viewing from an "ivory tower," regardless of one's achievements. Our community is composed of individuals who are earnest in their pursuit to forge meaningful connections and achieve significance in their endeavors.

The rapport between Dan and I blossomed due to our mutual belief in the principle that "significance breeds success," a notion that is not only the cornerstone of my organization but also a fundamental aspect of Daniel's Foundation Academies. This principle posits that the more people you assist and the more value you add to their lives, the greater the likelihood is of attaining your own goals. The approximately 1,500 members of the Orchestrated Connecting network are a testament to this approach, each aiming to positively impact the world in their unique ways. Despite their diverse methodologies and backgrounds, the profound connections they establish stem from a shared strategy toward business and life.

Success, a concept as elusive as it is sought after, becomes more attainable when approached through this lens. Living a life centered on making significant contributions to others—as Dan does and as promoted by Foundation Academies—creates a network of support and encouragement. This network, in turn, propels one towards personal and professional achievements. The narrative of success is thus rewritten not as a solitary climb to the top, but as a collective journey marked by shared struggles and triumphs.

The journeys of both Foundation Academies and Orchestrated Connecting LLC underlines the transformative *power of networking when infused with purpose and intention. It serves as a beacon for those who seek not only to ascend in their personal capacities but also to uplift those around them in meaningful ways. The philosophy that "significance breeds success" isn't merely theoretical but is vividly manifested in the lives of those impacted by Daniel Puder. He is a testament to the idea that true success comes not from what we accumulate for ourselves but from what we contribute to the lives of others. I am fortunate to call him a friend, an ally, and someone I'd leave my kids with.*

Life is short. In America, most of us may live into our eighties, which gives us billions of minutes to work with. Each one is precious, though. I've often heard people wonder what they would change if they could turn back time. This question usually reveals deep regrets of theirs, many of which they struggle to live with every day.

On the contrary, I've noticed during my travels in countries like India, Mexico, and parts of Peru that people there often have a greater sense of happiness than many in the more developed parts of the world. Despite having fewer material possessions, they don't obsess over happiness as if it's a rare resource they have to chase after, like we Americans often do.

This perspective has taught me that happiness and significance in life aren't about always seeking pleasure or personal gain. Instead, happiness and significance come from building relationships, contributing to the community, appreciating the nice moments every day, and living in a way that aligns with one's values. It's about understanding that every second is a chance to make an impact, not just on our own lives but on those around us. Living with intention and focusing on adding value wherever possible leads to a fulfilling and regret-free life.

Moments With Dad

My father, Brent Puder, has been the most significant

influence in my life. From my earliest memories, he instilled in me the values of hard work and perseverance. He was always there—playing with me, cheering me on at every sporting event, and supporting me through my challenges in school. Although my mother, Wanda Puder, a public school teacher and my favorite tutor, was incredibly supportive and loving, my connection with my father was different; he shaped my growth as a man.

As a child, my father would wrestle with me, much like I now do with my own son, Konrad. He may not have been an expert in wrestling techniques, but it wasn't about mastery. It was about the fun we had and the bond we built during those playful moments. As you now know, I faced significant challenges in school. The traditional model of sitting quietly for six to eight hours a day was particularly tough for me. Unlike the educational approaches in countries like Finland, Switzerland, and Sweden, where learning is integrated with play and designed to engage young minds actively, the system I was in didn't suit my learning style.

During those hard times, my father and mother were my rocks. I remember coming home overwhelmed and breaking down in tears, unable to handle the material in my assignments. He would sit down with me, helping me type up papers and craft essays, teaching me not just about the subject matter but about toughness and resourcefulness. He emphasized the importance of seeking help and building a supportive network—lessons that at the time were beyond my understanding, but that I would fully grasp later on.

Asking for help, they taught me, requires more courage than facing challenges alone. Vulnerability is a strength, not a weakness. This lesson became even clearer as I watched my dad manage his own company. With 30+ employees, he used their diverse skills to drive the company's success, creating a thriving business environment through teamwork and collaboration.

My folks have slowed down today; the joy of watching them interact with my son is immeasurable. They play together on the beach tossing a ball back and forth, their laughter reminding me of the memories I have of my own childhood with them. These moments are precious and a vivid reminder of the relationship we shared.

The lessons from my father have deeply influenced how I raise my own son and manage my relationships, both personal and professional. His example taught me that life's challenges are best met with a strong support system, and that true strength lies in the ability to seek help when needed. Through his actions, he showed me that a fulfilling life is built on a foundation of love, fun, and the willingness to be there for each other, values I try to teach Konrad today. I loved watching the bond between him and my dad. It reinforces how timeless the lessons were that he taught me.

Moments With Frank

I'd like to once again touch upon the influence Frank Shamrock had on my life. As you've read, I had the extraordinary opportunity to train at the American Kickboxing Academy beginning at 17, under the guidance of Frank, a renowned champion in the fighting world. Frank took a special interest in my potential and generously took me under his wing. He saw something in me that perhaps I hadn't fully recognized in myself at the time. One day, he even wrote on an 8x11 piece of paper that I could become a champ, a piece of paper I still have and cherish.

Frank wasn't just a coach. He was a mentor who invested in my growth as an athlete and as a person. At a time when he was at the peak of his career, having just won a championship fight against Tito Ortiz, Frank chose to guide me despite there being many other talented athletes in the gym. His decision to focus on my development was a pivotal moment in my life.

We spent countless hours together—training, traveling to fights, and just talking about life. These experiences were huge for me. Frank taught me not only the technical aspects of fighting but also how to understand and focus on my goals. He showed me a deeper sense of discipline and how to harness my potential to achieve results.

Most importantly, Frank inspired me to strive to become the best version of myself. At a critical time in my young life, his mentorship gave me the support and guidance I needed to realize my dreams in sports. Having a person like Frank in my corner, who was not only a top athlete but also a genuinely caring individual, was incredibly rare and something I am eternally grateful for.

Frank's influence on my life extended far beyond the gym. The lessons he taught me about dedication, understanding oneself, and pursuing excellence have stayed with me throughout my career and continue to impact me, even after my fighting days have finished.

Moments With Strangers

I always took pride in the little things when I was a mixed martial artist and when I was in the WWE. They say you never know what another person is going through, so always try to be kind. This saying can lead to plenty of significance if you take it upon yourself to brighten somebody's day, even with a ten-second interaction. A little moment in time you share with them that maybe, just maybe, made their day a little better.

One of my ways of doing this when I was fighting was to sign every single autograph I could after fights. Naturally, I'd show some preferential treatment towards the younger fans. I find that the younger someone is, the more potential events have for significance. Signing an autograph for an ecstatic seven-year-old could provide him with a memory to last a lifetime. So I'd usually sign the kids' memorabilia before the adults'. Each autograph and ensuing one- or two-sentence conversation with a wide-eyed child took me maybe 10 seconds. When it comes to significance, you and I can always afford 10 seconds.

Another set of little things I would do for young fans is set up fake arm wrestling and punching photos. I'd usually do this when I had a little more time to set up a photo-op. These kids had just seen me fly around the ring, doing my best to put on a show. Now they got the opportunity to lay one right on my chin, or take me down in an arm wrestling match. I was always pretty good at playing the heel, so I had no problem making it convincing for them. To this day, the collection of photos on my phone and computer is filled with shots of me losing armwrestling matches and getting popped in the face by smiling children, and you know what? Those are some of the most significant moments I captured as a professional athlete. When I was going through my pro-athletic career, fighting was fun and wrestling was fun, but impacting and influencing these young minds came with a level of fulfillment that couldn't be matched in the ring.

Whenever I visit a restaurant, I make it a point to ask the server their name and introduce myself. Often, I'll even shake their hand to show my respect and appreciation. Similarly, whenever I'm with my son and we see someone cleaning—whether they are part of our organization or working on the street or at another venue—I always make sure to thank them. I've taught my son that these individuals make the world a cleaner place. They deserve every bit of praise and gratitude you can give them. It's important to acknowledge and appreciate all the people who contribute to making society better.

In the end, our existence is broken down into little moments that combine to paint a portrait of our lives. I've found that, the more significant moments you can create for others, the more significant you become. This breeds success in whatever area you're looking for it in.

Little Moments, Big Influence

Throughout my life, several key figures have left a lasting impact on me. Starting from my youth, my pastor and various wrestling coaches shaped my early years, each teaching me different values and showing me the importance of gratitude, respect, and love.

One memory that vividly stands out involves, believe it or not, a teacher. Specifically, my second grade teacher, Mr. Star.

On his birthday, Mr. Star brought cookies for our class, a gesture that delighted everyone, especially a sweet-toothed, slightly chubby kid like me. Eager for a second cookie, I approached him and asked for a second one. He told me no. Confused, I pointed out that other kids in the class received an extra one. Mr. Star's reply was a lesson I've never forgotten. "It's because they said thank you, and you didn't." That moment taught me the incredible power of a simple 'thank you.' It wasn't just about manners; it was about acknowledging someone's kindness and the effort they made for you.

This lesson in gratitude stuck with me, and it's something I've really tried to stress with Konrad. Earlier this year, when somebody handed him something nice, he looked at them and said thank you. I believe being thankful shows you understand and acknowledge your blessings. It was wonderful to see him show these traits. Observing his interactions reminds me how significant it is to appreciate even the smallest gestures, and it's heartwarming to see others recognize this trait in him.

My parents played a monumental role in my upbringing, as you know. My father imparted various practical skills related to work, while my mother, a homemaker after years of teaching, excelled in the kitchen and raised us as a full-time stay-at-home mother. Every evening, she would cook for our family, involving my brother and me in the process. These cooking sessions created a sense of family and togetherness in us. I still have the cookbook case that was given to me from my mother, a memento filled with recipes and memories, symbolizing the significant influence she had in my life.

These experiences have taught me the importance of nurturing skills, expressing gratitude, and the impact of having positive role models. From learning the power of appreciation from Mr. Star to inheriting culinary skills from my mother, each lesson has contributed to who I am today. More importantly, they've allowed me to pass on these values to the next generation, ensuring that the lessons of significance continue to resonate and shape lives long into the future.

Growing up, my brother was a significant influence on

me. We shared countless moments that shaped both of us, from training together to being part of each other's lives in wrestling and beyond. Despite facing challenges at different stages, these experiences bonded us, even though they may have pushed us apart at points. Today, we both live in the same state and maintain a close relationship, speaking on a weekly basis, which continues to enrich my life. My brother is one of the leading psychiatrists in the world and has taught me a lot about life and the mind. He's given me plenty of ideas based on his area of expertise, and he inspires me with how he's always there for his kids and family. He shows me a little about what is possible in this world, and I am blessed to have him in my life.

Another major influence during my teenage years was my seventh and eighth-grade coach, Coach Lee. One memorable day, he challenged us to complete a thousand jumping jacks—a task that would test the limits of professional athletes, let alone middle schoolers. Coach Lee's rigorous training methods did not come from harshness, but from wanting to see us succeed. He instilled in us determination to never quit, training us to be tough and to win. Coach Lee believed in our potential.

Three more coaches of mine—Coach Matt, Coach Levens, and Coach Dan—played pivotal roles in advancing my wrestling skills, this time in high school. These men showed up and took a beating in order to wrestle us. They were tough and committed to making our team successful with their significance. Under their guidance, I not only improved as an athlete but also learned to push myself to new extremes.

Coach Levens met my son a few months ago. It was a blessing to be able to introduce my family to a man who impacted me for four years, every wrestling season. He dedicated so many hours to our team, not only in the wrestling gym and on the mat, but on a personal level. He used to have me over his house and built a friendship with me over my high school career. We are still friends today.

Each of these individuals—my parents, my teachers, my brother, and my coaches—contributed uniquely to my development. They taught me the value of hard work, the importance of perseverance, and the strength that comes from genuine support. These lessons were taught in the tiniest of moments that would have huge significance for me later on. Never underestimate how important your actions and words can be, no matter how small they seem. The lessons these people taught me have stayed with me, guiding me in my ongoing journey both inside and outside of sports.

Moments in Business and Sports

In my journey to open up schools across the country, I came across many important people who influenced the future of our company. One of these people was Luis Marcelino, a remarkable friend and now a business partner, who played a huge role right from the start. Luis's commitment to our vision—enhancing the lives of children through education—was vital, especially when our resources were limited.

Luis not only embraced our mission but actively expanded our network through his connections. He introduced me to Jose Flores, a renowned motivational speaker who we partnered with for our school in Oakland Park, Florida, along with many other influential figures. His proactive approach of setting up meetings and phone calls with the Broward County and West Palm Beach Police Departments, various schools, counselors, and professional athletes saved us years of developmental time. With a mere phone call or text, Luis would bridge gaps that seemed insurmountable. He gave our projects life and helped transform potential into reality.

Another important relationship was with Harlan Gittin, a mentor who opened my eyes to new possibilities. Meeting Harlan at an event, I was shown a world that was much different than the one I was used to. Harlan, a successful businessman I mentioned in Chapter 6, demonstrated that significance could extend beyond business. Despite his immense wealth, Harlan was grounded and committed to using his resources for the greater good. His philosophy was that improving others' lives inevitably leads to personal fulfillment. He was under no obligation to make any connections for me or invite me anywhere. It did not serve his business in any way. What it did help was his level of significance. His higher being. Harlan Gittin is my practical blueprint for applying success to meaningful causes.

Harlan's network was impactful, to say the least. He introduced me to Harvey Vecherey, who would become a key supporter of our educational initiatives. When I launched our first school, Harvey and his wife made an important investment in MLMPI Prep Academy, now known as Foundation Academies. Their loan helped us weather the crucial first year, when many businesses go under. We were able to pay their investment back in just a year and a half. Harvey remains an integral part of our company. He embodies the impact of significant relationships in business.

I can't mention people who were significant in the early stages of Foundation Academies without mentioning Joseph D'Alba. D'Alba is a retired lawyer and one of my initial partners. He played a crucial role in the early days of our venture by not only providing financial support, which we have since repaid in full, but also offering invaluable advice, direction, and mentorship. His guidance was important for both my personal development and for the strategic growth of our company.

I also had the fortune early on of meeting Joe Sauma in New Jersey at a family office conference in New Hampshire, named Opal. During our meeting, Joe jokingly asked for one of those "punch in the face" pictures I mentioned earlier that I used to take with kids. We were fast friends, and this foundation has led to a very fruitful partnership for the both of us.

Shortly after meeting him, Joe's family office invested in building more schools around America. He told me, "Go change the world, kid." This support greatly boosted our efforts to expand Foundation Academies. Over the past few years, Joe has not only given us financial backing but has also become a business mentor to me. His wisdom knows no bounds, and he's even taken the time to get to know me on a personal level. All of this has only made our collaboration stronger, and I can't wait to see what we can come up with in the future.

Although I didn't always meet the best people while I was in the WWE, there were still tremendous men and women in that company who I keep in touch with to this day. One of them is Gangrel. While in the WWE at the Ohio Valley wrestling training facility, I met Gangrel, whose real name is David Heath. He was one of the most amazing wrestlers and humans I've ever met, trained with, and built a friendship with. If you Google his past and what he's gone through, you'll find he's overcome many different challenges in his personal and professional life. Today, he is in love with his amazing wife, owns a wrestling school in South Florida, and still wrestles.

One of the first times I really saw the quality of his character was when we went to the Shriners Children's Hospital in Kentucky to go see some kids and put smiles on their faces. When leaving the hospital, a few people recognized us in the elevator and told us what was going on with their little sister. There was a house fire and the girl inhaled a lot of smoke, which did a number on her lungs. For weeks she wouldn't say much and wouldn't get excited about anything in her life. When we walked through the door and her parents announced who was there to see her, though, she looked over and immediately made her first joyful expressions in weeks, specifically directed at David. He may have been a terror in the ring, but Gangrel was one of the sweetest and most genuine people I ever met in the industry.

It's amazing to be able to see someone create a celebrity personality, build it over time, and utilize it for good. David influenced so many people even if he was with them for only a minute. He has a heart of gold. Within his wrestling school he creates significance with tons of students who are trying to make a name for themselves. He coaches and supports their personal and professional growth in this world, not just as wrestlers.

Senator Steve Smith is one of my good friends in Arizona. He is bright, intelligent, caring, and passionate for what he believes in. He is a retired state senator in the Phoenix, Arizona area who cares about his faith in God, our youth, and the future of education. He has impacted people's lives within the school choice world, his community, and the nation by working with different foundations and helping change policies. Since I've known him, beginning in about 2010, laws and regulations have drastically changed in the state of Arizona, and we are infinitely excited for the start of our Mike Tyson-backed school in the fall of 2023. He was a huge help by opening doors and getting us in front of the right people, all while never asking for anything in return. His significance will impact generations.

The Honorable William Chatfield has worked for multiple presidents of the United States. He was a director of the Selective Service for one president and has worked honorably in Washington D.C. over the last 60+ years of his life. He introduced me to multiple people in D.C. and other places over the years who were great Americans and have impacted the policies that will shape the next generation of civilians. I'm blessed to have somebody like him in my life who has taken the time to have lunch and dinner with me to discuss these matters. He has also opened plenty of doors for me.

I talk about Ed Connors, a giant in the health and fitness industry who is largely responsible for the development of Gold's Gym, all the time. This one man has supported over 500 amateur and professional athletes by giving them a place to live when they need one, along with feeding and supporting them with a free gym membership. Some of these athletes include John Cena and Jay Cutler. If you look at who's who in the fitness world today, odds are, Ed has positively influenced them in some way.

I've been fortunate enough to stay at his house once when I was traveling. He even mentioned me in his book about his business exploits, The Three Muscleteers, which was a thrill for me. I've really enjoyed spending time with him over the last 20 years, learning about who he is as a human being, and soaking in as much advice as I can. At one point, I needed $3,000 for a loan while I was going through hard times. I went to him and he didn't think twice about loaning me the money, which I paid back as soon as I could. He's now stayed at my house and spent time with my family and friends. Having people like Ed Connors in your life is why I always stress to seek out the best mentors and teachers you can.

Nelson F. Hincapie has been a believer in me since I first moved to South Florida. I first met Nelson at a coffee shop through a mutual friend, about eight years ago while he was the CEO of Voices for Children and I was running my non-profit. Since then, he has become the President of the Miami-Dade College Foundation. He has introduced me to so many impactful people, given me advice, and supported my vision to impact our next generation. If you ever want to watch a really good TED Talk, check his out. It's called "A Broken Childhood Inspires Purpose."

My experiences with these people, both big and small, have taught me lessons about the power of community and mentorship in entrepreneurship. The success of our schools does not just prove that our vision was a good one, but also that the effort of everyone involved was well-spent. Each person who supported us not only accelerated our progress but also showed that teamwork is essential if you want to create a lasting impact.

The journey also revealed the importance of gratitude. In a world often driven by individual achievement, the success of our schools shows how shared goals and support can lead to incredible results. It is a reminder that no moment or effort is too small, and no contribution is insignificant when it's in line with a noble purpose.

Whether in education or any other field, the concepts of mutual support, mentorship, and community involvement hold the key to not just personal success but also to creating a culture where everyone can thrive. These principles have built our educational philosophy and continue to inspire our daily operations and future goals. We will always embrace these values as we continue to build an educational model that builds up young minds and prepares them for a promising future.

I'm blessed for all the significant moments I've

experienced. Every relationship I mentioned began with a small moment in time that would go on to change my life. They are some of the reasons why I believe significance breeds success in life. Each one of these mentors or coaches has given me a perspective of significance and what is possible. My only hope is that I can be as significant for them as they have been for me.

Puder's Journal on Significant Moments

My challenge for you is to list two or three people who have made a big influence in your life, then try to copy that influence in someone else's life. For instance, the little moments my father had with me when I was a kid, wrestling, helping me with homework, etc., I have tried to replicate with my son. Try and take someone under your wing if they don't know how to do something as well as you can, like Frank Shamrock did. You'll be shocked at the impact you can have on this world.

Who are some significant people in your life?

_____
_____
_____
_____
_____

How can you be similarly significant to someone else?

_____
_____
_____
_____
_____
_____

Chapter 8: Learning Significance

I didn't fully understand the concept of significance breeding success until I was in my 30s. The foundation, though, was laid much earlier by influential people during my childhood, like my coaches, youth group leaders, and family you've heard stories of. My grandmother, who I haven't mentioned yet, introduced me to the ideals of serving others and adding value to their lives, which are essential if you want to have a meaningful existence.

One of the most important people in my early life was my grandmother, who I nicknamed "Grandma Knockout." This funny nickname was also a testament to her strong, impactful presence. She was both a gentle and formidable person. From a young age, she helped teach me the importance of caring and generosity. Visits to her house were some of the highlights of my childhood, filled with the warmth of her kitchen and the sweetness of the treats she loved to give me. She was always nurturing to me and my brother. Her spirit made her home a place of comfort and joy.

During my senior year of high school, certain circumstances allowed me to experience daily life with her. My family moved 40 minutes south, but I chose to stay and finish high school where I grew up. Grandma Knockout offered me a room and that was where I stayed that year, which deepened our bond. Living with her meant I got to experience her peaceful and kind soul every day, which was a delight. She cherished talking about her family history, her beloved dog, and enjoyed leisurely walks around the neighborhood. These simple joys showed me what life well-lived looked like. My grandmother emphasized relationships and personal connections over material possessions, which is how I now try to live.

As time passed, Grandma Knockout faced several health challenges, including a broken hip. Despite these issues, the closeness we developed during my senior year never wore off. Whenever she was hospitalized, no matter where I was living at the time, I made it a point to be the first grandchild by her side. We had a deep bond and I wanted her to always know what she meant to me.

When I got home one day while this was starting to happen, I noticed a flier for a retirement home on the table, which my mother had left out. Curious, I asked her about it, and she explained that they were considering it for my grandmother. In that moment, I felt compelled to stand by my grandmother, so I told my mother, "Whatever you do for her, I'll do for you." In this case, that meant I was going to send them to a home as well when the time came. This made my parents reflect on their decision, and it worked. They moved my grandmother into their home instead of a retirement facility.

A couple of years later, the idea of moving her to a retirement home propped back up. Once again, I spoke to them about my commitment to copy whatever decision they made regarding her care. They had to reconsider once again. My mother ended up dedicating a lot of time and effort to care for my grandmother at home, which was incredibly significant. My grandmother needed family support more than anything at that stage of her life.

My grandmother's attitude during this time was truly remarkable. Despite her health challenges, whenever anyone asked how she was doing in the hospital, she would respond with a cheerful "pretty good." This positive outlook was impressive considering the circumstances. Many people tend to be negative when facing difficulties, but my grandmother maintained a positive attitude throughout it all.

This taught me that significance in life isn't just about the actions we take to help others; it's also about how we conduct ourselves. You can be responsible for many kind acts, but if you have a negative attitude or behave poorly in other moments, those actions might not resonate as meaningfully. My grandmother had a spirit of genuine kindness and optimism, never letting her tougher moments dampen things. Even as her life was nearing its end, she remained upbeat and content.

The time I spent with her, both in the hospital and during my childhood playing in parks, left a profound impact on me. It showed me how one can live a life of significance through consistent kindness and a perpetually positive outlook. Her example continues to inspire me to strive for the same level of graciousness and impact in my own life.

Her example taught me how significant unconditional love could be. She supported and cared for others without expecting anything in return. She consistently went above and beyond for anyone in need, personifying the belief that significance in life comes from how we help and relate to people. Her approach to life was a lesson in the power of selfless love and the importance of being present for those around us.

I learned from her that the core of living a significant life is in the small acts of kindness and understanding that we extend to others. This has affected how I view relationships and community aid. Every interaction is an opportunity to leave a positive imprint on someone's life, meaning no gesture of kindness is too small, and every moment of connection with another human being counts.

Having learned all these important lessons from her, I try my best to live my life like she would have wanted me to. This is how I honor her. Her core values of unconditional love, relentless support, and genuine care for others are cornerstones in my approach to relationships. They remind me that our legacy is built through the love we share and the support we offer. Every day is an opportunity to contribute positively to the world around us.

A Significant Life

Learning the concept of significance can be hard, especially in a world where most people seek to live out their personal ambitions, first and foremost. They focus on building businesses, pursuing dreams, or traveling the world, and forget to ponder the most important question: after achieving all this, what is life truly about? Many people reach high levels of success—financially, and/or physically—yet still find themselves searching for something more, something to fill a hole in their spirit that material possessions can't fill.

This pursuit of success can lead to a cycle where no amount of money or luxury is enough. Even if you eat at fine restaurants or drive nicer cars, the appeal of these things eventually fades away. This is not a significant life. True significance comes from actions that positively affect others and contribute to the world. Simply having a good day personally does not necessarily mean you've lived a day of significance. Did your actions make the world a better place? Have you impacted others in a meaningful way?

I believe a lot of this is tied into our perspectives, interpretations, and beliefs. I have learned how to shift my viewpoint in order to see things through other people's eyes, to a degree. Not everyone can or wants to live this way, however. A significant life, just like in The Matrix, offers a red and blue pill. Which one do you choose?

Significance should be viewed as a lifestyle—a conscious choice to live a life based on values, vision, and purpose for others. It's about building a foundation that no one can take away and standing firm in those beliefs no matter the challenges. These challenges can strengthen our commitment to our values, much like the physical challenges a person faces in the gym. Many start the year with resolutions to improve their fitness, yet give up when the going gets tough, unable to get past the discomfort and stay true to their goals.

As I've gotten older, I realize that significance is a combination of what we give to the world and how we choose to live our lives. It's about trying to be better each day, and not just for ourselves, but for the collective good. It means being tough in the face of adversity, compassionate in the face of hardship, and generous in the face of need.

The challenge of living a life of significance is similar to getting through a difficult workout. You have to push through the initial pain and fatigue in order to reach a stronger, more fulfilled state. Just as muscles grow stronger through stress, our ability to be significant strengthens as we consistently apply our values through actions.

Understanding and living a life of significance is an ongoing journey. By choosing to act with purpose and integrity, we can forge a path that leads not only to personal success, but to a richer, more rewarding life that leaves a lasting impact on the world.

Puder's Journal About Learning Significance

I challenge you to look at how you learn and what your core beliefs are today. What do you stand for? If I asked someone what you were about, what would you want them to say? Write them down below, then decide how you're going to live out these beliefs in the future. One quote I often hear is "how you do one thing is how you do everything." My challenge for you is to stop talking about being someone who adds value to other people's lives, and start becoming one.

What are your learning styles? (This will help you learn how to learn)

_____

_____
_____
_____
_____

What are your core beliefs?

_____
_____
_____
_____
_____

Are there any beliefs that do not serve your vision and/or purpose?

_____
_____
_____
_____
_____
_____
_____

Pick which beliefs you align with. How are you living out these beliefs? If you aren't embodying now, how do you plan to?

_____
_____
_____
_____
_____
_____
_____

Chapter 9: Finding Your Alley

I'm going to hit you with a hard truth here: there are only so many things you're good at. If you haven't figured that out yet, I assure you, life will teach you eventually. This is what makes us unique! I can't do a lot of the things my fellow Foundation Academies partners like Jenn Kramer, Q, Brittney Sharpe, or Mike Williams do. And they can't do a lot of the things I do. We make a great team when you put us all together, though. Why? Because we've all been able to find our alley.

I won't say the name of the person I'm about to tell you a story about, but rest assured, you know who he is. I first met this man through the athletic world back when I was a signed MMA fighter. He is a major celebrity in the health and fitness world, so he happened to be at the same event. I asked him to film a Public Service Announcement for our non-profit, and for part of this, he was required to read lines off a teleprompter.

I noticed pretty quickly that he was having trouble getting through them. I didn't want to embarrass him, but eventually I had no choice but to stop the script reading to get to the bottom of it. I pulled him aside and asked if we needed to feed him the script in a different way. He looked at me and said, "I'm dyslexic," I then asked if he was put in learning disability classes as a child like I was. He said he was. We both laughed;

this was a big connection point for us. We didn't have to say what each of us was thinking, because we both knew. We were thinking something to the effect of, "And look at us now!"

I found my alley and he found his, then we developed those talents so that we could get over the pain of how hard school was when we were growing up, and how cruel our classmates were at times. All of that hard work pays off when you find your niche, you're driven, and you put good people around you. I've met so many athletes, entrepreneurs, and successful people in this world who push so hard because of past experiences. Most of the time they are out to prove people wrong. It fuels them to the point where they cannot rest until they reach the finish line.

He and I both struggled in the classroom. Not because we weren't smart, but because we learned differently than most of our classmates, and the schooling systems we were exposed to didn't have the proper framework in place to accommodate us. My teachers and counselors quickly labeled me learning disabled and put me in special ed classes. School was something that I needed help in, though they didn't understand the proper route for my learning style. They lumped me in with every other student who struggled in the classroom for whatever reason, thinking that, if I just get a little more time to process things and maybe receive the curriculum in a simpler way, it would all work itself out. It doesn't really work like that.

The traditional schooling system is only meant for certain types of people. I'm referring to people with the concentration to sit for eight hours a day and are adept at taking and processing directions. Partially using my own struggles as inspiration, we created Foundations Academy with a five-hour daily schedule, all while taking in the same amount of content. Our students learn how to build and be a part of teams. We teach them how to learn how to learn, adjust to different learning styles and love languages, develop soft and hard skills, and help our students understand what they want to build in their lives.

Labeling someone as having a learning disability and placing them in special ed classes, which kids will automatically judge as being inferior, can potentially ruin their schooling careers, which has far-reaching implications for the rest of their lives. It is belittling. It is humiliating. Most of my classmates who were in these classes with me were also told they were simply different, and that's why they were there. We were never taught about our differing learning styles of love languages, or taught how to work on what we're good at. We were just informed on what we weren't good at.

I don't believe life is about what you're not good at. Being successful in life, or being significant, is about understanding your alley. Find what you are good at and find the right people to surround yourself with in order to construct the best team possible.

Think about if a football team only had offensive linemen for every single position. Or if a soccer team only had goalies. Avoiding this mistake is one of the most important tasks of a CEO or President of an organization. It is his or her job to find the right people for the right positions, all of whom should be smarter than himself or herself. When I first started Foundation Academies I wore many hats out of necessity. But today, I can define my role as having a basic understanding of the inner workings of each department, while knowing the right people and the right questions to ask in order to get the job done. This helps me hire the right people and build the best systems possible. My job as President of Foundation Academies is to oversee and build on the business, not necessarily to run it. There's a difference between the two, which is a topic for a book I will write in the future.

Going back to the fitness icon I mentioned, he and I would have benefited from Foundation Academies' alternative curriculum, which presents content in a variety of ways so that different types of learners can grasp it. It turns out, the struggles I faced as a student made me a better educator. Imagine that! What if this fitness icon would have equated his failures in school to the rest of his life? You learned in Chapter 3 that every "failure" is a chance to learn. But this is a nuanced way of looking at things that most children can't comprehend yet.

If this person would have looked at his awful grades and how he was falling behind the rest of his classmates and friends and thought, wow, I must just be a loser, what then? We likely would never have heard of one of the preeminent figures in the history of the fitness industry.

What did he do instead? The same thing I did. He realized that, unfortunately, he wasn't going to be academically inclined, at least not in the traditional sense. There would be no valedictorian speeches or Ivy League acceptance letters in his future. Instead, he'd have to scratch and claw his way through school, while simultaneously developing what was and is his God-given ability: being incredibly strong, athletic, and aesthetic. He also signed some of the biggest contracts in the fitness industry and likely has one of the highest net worths ever for this field.

I believe everyone has two or three traits that separate them from most of their peers. No one is utterly without any sort of talent. The trick is to find what your true calling is, then pursue it with every ounce of your being. Find your alley. Mine was athletics and branding myself, then it was in the nonprofit world, then it was building for-profit companies as a social entrepreneur. These are the domains in which I have decided to pour all my energy into.

Peter Drucker

Peter Drucker was a famous educator, author, and consultant of the 20th century, who was one of the pioneers of modern management theory. In other words, how people and businesses should operate in order to be successful. He wrote an essay in the late-90s for the *Harvard Business Review* that was later published in book-form. It was called *Managing Oneself*. In it, he lays out a game plan on how someone can find his or her strengths, then maximize them as a professional. One of his core taglines was, "Do what you do best and outsource the rest." I made it mandatory for all Foundation Academies staff members in our headquarters to read this book, because I believe it has some timeless lessons that people like myself and the fitness celebrity I mentioned have unknowingly employed. The following is a small excerpt from *Managing Oneself*:

"One cannot build performance on weaknesses, let alone on something one cannot do at all. Throughout history, people had little need to know their strengths. A person was born into a position and a line of work: The peasant's son would also be a peasant; the artisan's daughter, an artisan's wife; and so on. But now people have choices. We need to know our strengths in order to know where we belong. The only way to discover your strengths is through feedback analysis."

Every word of that, from what I've seen in my life, is true. I could have worked my butt off to become an above average reader and writer, which was my biggest challenge as a student. But for what? At the very best, I would have gone from being well below average to slightly below average. The same goes for the aforementioned health and fitness celebrity who struggled with dyslexia. What industries give you the biggest potential for significance based on your strengths? Once you find them, you've also found your alley.

Delegation and outsourcing are critical strategies for growth, especially in the startup phase. When building our online platform, puder.ai, we opted to work with a tech team from India. This decision was cost-effective and yielded a high-quality product. Outsourcing to countries with lower labor costs allows you to hire a team for the same price as a single domestic employee. This scales your operational capacity while also maintaining the quality you want.

Startups increasingly rely on outsourcing to manage initial costs effectively. This strategy allows young companies to have control over a big portion of their equity while continuing to grow. Outsourcing can involve basically any service, from customer support and technical development to content creation and administrative tasks. However, managing the person or people you've hired as an outsource option requires a lot of oversight. You have to make sure they are aligning with your business standards and goals, or else you're just wasting money.

Foundation Academies has also taken steps to optimize our supply chain by working directly with manufacturers. This approach reduces costs by eliminating the middleman and lets us have more control over the production process. Whether it's sourcing materials for products or negotiating with service providers, a direct relationship with a manufacturer can mean big-time savings and improved product quality.

Developing Skills

While I was still an MMA fighter, I vividly remember a pivotal moment before a bout at the HP Pavilion in San Jose, California. Standing beside my coach, in gorilla position, a question that I had been thinking about just came out of me: "Why do I fight?" His response had a hint of sarcasm in it. "Because you don't want a real job." Javier Mendez and others around me were well aware of my keen interest in business ventures beyond the ring. I was always hustling—securing sponsors, organizing networking events, and exploring various money-making ventures. Even though fighting provided a solid foundation for publicity and brand-building, I loved the business and marketing side of my career.

Still, the ring was my main focus and where I dedicated the lion's share of my time towards. Anything less than that, in this arena, leads to some not-so-good results.

Developing any skill set requires considerable effort and time. People say mastery in any field requires at least 10,000 hours of practice. To put that into perspective, if you worked a full-time job for five years, that would roughly equate to those 10,000 hours. Looking back on my athletic career, I estimate I invested over 25,000 hours in training and competition. It didn't go to waste; at 26 years old, certain publications had me ranked as the 26th best heavyweight MMA fighter in the world.

Now, let's dive into how I honed my skills in the fighting

arena before looking into my entrepreneurship. Shockingly, I never enjoyed the parts of fighting that involved getting punched, kicked, or beaten up daily. Can you believe it? However, this inevitable part of the job made me learn quickly. I focused on mastering defensive tactics like keeping my hands up, strengthening my body to withstand punishment, and moving in ways that minimized hits. Learning to absorb the impact during training sessions was crucial.

The key to developing my fighting was in surrounding myself with top-notch trainers and fighters. Success in the fight game hinges on three main parts. The first is having the wisdom and skills necessary to understand the intricacies of fighting. The second involves building your athletic ability. And the third is to build a personal brand outside the cage.

This approach not only helped my career in the fighting world, but also laid the groundwork for my ventures outside of it. Each punch absorbed and each round survived taught me resilience and adaptability—traits that were also valuable in business. My journey through fighting and entrepreneurship shows how skills and lessons from one space can lead to success in another, even if they don't seem to have anything in common.

Navigating the world of combat sports is as much about finding the right mentors and coaches as it is about physical training. In a sport that tends to attract people dealing with personal challenges like anger or past trauma, it can be difficult to find guidance that can enhance both your physical ability and personal growth.

In my journey, I was fortunate to connect with mentors like Javier Mendez and Frank Shamrock who helped shape my career. They weren't just coaches; they were guides in the early and crucial stages of my fighting life. They put me through the ringer when it came to training, but they also inspired me to pursue greatness in all aspects of life.

Physical and technical training only form part of the equation. Mental and emotional resilience are equally important. I urge every fighter to work with a sports psychologist or a counselor who knows about the unique psychological demands of professional athletics. The mental battles that fighters face are relentless. Having the support of a good psychologist can make a huge difference, especially considering the mental strains that come with the sport.

Many fighters excel in the ring but struggle with life outside of it, often because of a lack of financial knowledge or life skills. It's a sad reality that some of the most talented fighters end up broke once their bodies can't handle mixed martial arts anymore. They lack the necessary support to manage their success.

That's why having a holistic support system is crucial. This system should include coaches who focus not just on physical success but also on building mental strength and emotional health. Having a good legacy in fighting requires more than just winning matches; it means you've made good life choices, managed your finances wisely, and planned for the future.

The path to becoming a successful professional fighter is complex and multifaceted. It involves more than just determination and physical strength. You also need mental resilience, strategic thinking, and a support system that includes both technical trainers and mental health professionals. If they embrace the physical and psychological parts of training, fighters can have success in and out of the ring.

Once you've mastered the physical and psychological aspects of fight training, it's important to tackle the business side of your career. I suggest taking a course—online or at a community college—to understand basic business concepts. You can also sit down with business owners locally and pick their brains on how they make the right decisions, something I've done a lot in my career. Understanding these things help you avoid some of the dangers of being a professional fighter with a little bit of money to his name. You don't want to be taken advantage of via a bad contract like I was, and you want to have a reasonable budget for your lifestyle. These skills will go on to serve you in many other areas of your life.

Start by learning how to create a business plan or

executive summary. This document outlines your goals, strategies, and how you plan to achieve them. It's your roadmap, guiding you from where you are now to where you want to be. Next, get familiar with financial budgets. Managing your finances effectively is critical, especially in a career where earnings can be unpredictable. Learning to budget helps you maintain financial stability and plan for both short-term needs and long-term goals.

Third, develop a financial forecast model. This tool helps you predict future earnings, expenses, and profitability. Understanding forecasting allows you to make good decisions and prepare for different financial scenarios.

Finally, focus on branding and designing your image within your industry, all while looking to future market trends. Successful people like Jeff Bezos and Elon Musk didn't just excel in their fields—they anticipated the movement of different markets and adapted their strategies accordingly. They prepared themselves for emerging technologies like artificial intelligence, robotics, and augmented reality to keep their edge and drive their businesses forward.

Finance Basics

I'm now going to dive deeper into some of these topics, giving you insight on how to apply these principles in order to build a personal or business brand. This knowledge isn't just about fighting—it's about building a sustainable career and making good decisions that align with future market opportunities and your professional goals.

An executive summary is a crucial document that outlines your vision, identifies problems, presents solutions, and introduces your team or yourself. It gives an overview of who you are and what you aim to achieve. To start crafting your own, you can find various executive summary templates online. Messing around with different templates will help you understand how to best communicate the essence of your business to others.

114

Following the executive summary, the business plan goes more in depth, introducing analysis of market strategies and future factors. For instance, a colleague of mine recently prepared to launch a company with a comprehensive 76-page business plan. It outlined every aspect of the business operations and objectives. I was really impressed by the amount of planning that went into it, and how clear his vision for the company was.

Understanding finances is another important skill. By examining budgets, you can gauge monthly costs and determine how much you need to sell your product or service to maintain a profit. When I was a fighter, I didn't grasp these financial details as well as I do now, which is why I emphasize their importance. Learning about finances early on will help you manage your business's cash flow—a common downfall for many businesses that leads to failure eventually. My father once told me that the lifeline of the company is cash flow. Another mentor of mine told me it's not how much you make, but how much you spend, save, or invest. Whether you're a business owner or just an employee, at some point you learn that most people in life are not disciplined about their finances. If you choose to be disciplined, you will be more prepared for life.

This information is not just about keeping your business and/or personal brand afloat. It is also about ensuring it thrives. By understanding these core business elements—from your executive summary to detailed financial planning—you can confidently get over many challenges you used to think were too complicated. This chapter aims to give you a solid foundation in these areas, setting the stage for successful business management and growth.

Hiring Basics

I took on numerous business endeavors when I was younger, many of which you've learned about. But I quickly realized that I didn't understand how organizational structures worked. This was highlighted when I launched a nonprofit in

2010. In an impulsive moment on TMZ, I declared my intention to visit schools and confront bullies to protect kids who were being bullied. I'm thankful I did this because it sent me along this path that has been the most rewarding and significant experience of my life. But in reality, I was in over my head in starting this nonprofit without any of the skills I just highlighted. Acknowledging that, basically, I didn't know what I was doing was instrumental in the early years of my nonprofit. It led to me establishing a good foundation by putting the right people around me (remember what Peter Drucker said about delegation?)

We were all driven by a clear purpose, which helped us develop effective programming and curriculums that could make a sustainable, multi-generational impact.

As I switched over to the school sector, I applied the lessons learned from my early experiences with our nonprofit. I knew that success in this arena meant I had to collaborate with partners who had a deeper knowledge base than my own. This strategy is a universal principle across all industries. The myth of the "self-made" individual is just that—a myth. True progress comes from collaboration.

For anyone wanting to be an entrepreneur, do not skimp on choosing your team. Take your time, do your research, network as much as you can, and make the best choices possible. Your team should include people who bring a diverse set of skills and perspectives:

Technical Expert: Someone who knows all about the science or technology of your industry.

Business Strategist: A visionary who understands market trends and can guide you through complex landscapes.

Operational Manager: A leader capable of building and optimizing a team to perform at its best.

We have clearly defined these roles among my

Foundation Academies partners. We always try to improve by adding industry experts into our leadership group. This helps our operation be as innovative and effective as possible.

Business Owner Traits and Tips

One crucial lesson I've learned is that no one excels at everything. The belief that you can is not only false but potentially harmful to personal growth and business success. My goal has always been to surround myself with people who are smarter in specific areas than I am. This gives me the opportunity to constantly learn. Both the business and I benefit from a wide range of knowledge and experience.

This approach requires you to be humble, with a good understanding of your strengths and weaknesses. A good leader knows the importance of building a team that complements his or her skills, while also filling the gaps in their knowledge base. This creates a good culture and pushes the business forward, for the team has enough collective expertise to handle pretty much any challenge.

A leader should also excel in people management, have a forward-looking vision for the market, and the ability to put the right people in the right roles. These skills are important when you're trying to create an innovative and productive workplace, where every team member can thrive.

Ultimately, the true test of a leader is not just in achieving personal success but in contributing to the improvement of the team and the community it serves. I do my best to live out this idea as a business owner. I try to add value to the lives of others, and in doing so, I find a deeper, more fulfilling measure of success.

For anyone starting out or looking to expand their knowledge in a specific field, using the wealth of information available online is invaluable. Tools like Google, TikTok (for now), Instagram, and ChatGPT are treasure troves of resources where you can search for specific terms related to your interests. While the internet is flooded with both high-quality information and misleading content, over time you'll develop the ability to identify which sources are legitimate and which are not.

When you come across individuals whose work resonates with your goals, reaching out to them via social media can be a game-changer. These professionals often have public profiles and host their own events, or offer mentorship opportunities. Engaging with them by offering your help or showing genuine interest in their work can lead to valuable connections. Instead of directly asking for favors, offer something valuable in return. This could be in the form of assistance at an event or a donation to a cause they care about, which can help forge a lasting relationship.

Participating actively in events, especially those where you can interact directly with influencers and leaders in your field, is another good tactic. If possible, invest in VIP tickets to these events or contribute to their initiatives. This not only gives you access to exclusive networking opportunities, but also creates a base for a relationship because of mutual respect and shared interests.

Building a successful business or career in sports is not just about individual talent or having a groundbreaking idea. It involves cultivating a deep understanding of your field, connecting with the right people, and effectively managing resources. By embracing learning, fostering relationships, and using the right amount of external resources, you can get over the challenges of any industry. You can make huge strides toward achieving your goals.

The core of learning to live significantly is understanding that life is not just about personal achievements but also about how we enrich the lives of others. This understanding transforms our attitudes as business owners into more meaningful ones, creating a legacy that transcends our own and helps future generations thrive.

Puder's Journal on Finding Your Alley

I'm going to give you three simple pieces of a framework for your business, many of which I've already covered in this book:

1. Create your business vision. What sort of company are you envisioning running? How will your company change or improve an industry? What does the future of the industry look like?

2. Create your life vision. How do you imagine your life will look in five years? Ten years? Thirty years? And not just you personally; create a vision for a family, if you'd like to build one.

3. Find your mission. What do you and your business partners want to accomplish in the first year? What about in three years? What are some actionable items you can tackle immediately to facilitate this process?

If you think this way of life might be the right fit for you, commit to it completely. 90% won't cut it. Would you tolerate a significant other of yours being unfaithful 10% of the time? You are doing your partners a disservice by not pouring all of your possible effort into whatever venture you convince them to join you on. Similarly, they must also be completely invested in building something. It's never easy to let someone go, but I've had to do it many times over the years because someone simply didn't buy into what we were trying to accomplish, and this was reflected in the results they produced, or didn't produce. Take some time to think about what you want out of the alley you choose before filling out the lines below, or wherever you write your thoughts down on.

What is your vision for your business, today and in the future?

_____

_____

_____

_____

_____

_____

What is your life vision, today and in the future?

_____

_____

_____

_____

_____

What is your mission? (your mission should broken up into goals and tasks)

_____

_____

_____

_____

_____

_____

Chapter 10: Time to Build

The phrase "a time to build" carries huge significance beyond just finding a job or pursuing a career. It means you're in a period of creating something lasting and impactful, whether for yourself or a broader community. For many, it suggests the old-school path: attend college, secure employment, and follow the steps towards personal and professional fulfillment (get promoted, get married, have kids, etc.). But what does it genuinely mean to build? Is it just about having financial stability, or is there more to it?

For me, building Foundation Academies has been a multifaceted journey stretching across the last two decades. It began with my professional fighting career at the age of 19 when I debuted as a pro fighter in Japan. I also launched Puder Strength Training at the time, a business that was supposed to be a nonprofit. That summer, I led a youth strength training program, blending physical fitness with personal development. This experience was not only pivotal for my athletic career, due to the exposure it gave me, but it also gave me some foundational skills I would later use to build Foundation Academies.

Transitioning out of fighting marked a huge pivot in my life. The world of mixed martial arts is as brutal as it is straightforward. There are mental, physical, emotional, and spiritual challenges you have to face every day. Taking punches and kicks from some of the sport's best was a routine that eventually made me assess my life's direction. Why go through so much pain? What made me get up each morning and face this adversity?

These experiences made me build a resilient spirit and improved focus. The physical demands of fighting taught me the essence of grit and the importance of a good foundation. However, the literal skills of fighting—striking, grappling, and overpowering opponents—don't have much utility in the real world. Rarely does anyone appreciate the skills of a fighter outside the ring. You can get in a lot of trouble for that type of thing, believe it or not!

The non-fighting qualities I developed through my career—discipline, resilience, and the ability to overcome discomfort—are universal, though. I learned to rise each day, regardless of pain or challenges. I had a clear vision and purpose. This mindset allowed me to push beyond my boundaries.

My fighting career also showed me the importance of teamwork. Success in life, much like in sports, is never a solo trip. It involves collaborating with the right people who share your vision and commitment. People who want to help you. Building anything of value, whether a business, a community project, or a personal goal, relies on the effort of a dedicated team, whether you acknowledge it or not.

Today, as I've moved forward from the worlds of Mixed Martial Arts and the WWE to business and philanthropy, the lessons I learned in the ring are ingrained in everything I do. The fight world taught me more than how to throw a punch; it taught me how to build a life of significance, how to construct a team capable of huge achievements, and how to create a legacy of purpose. As I continue to grow, these lessons are the guiding light of my journey, pointing me in the right direction as I help others build their paths to success. Building, at its core, is about more than just personal achievement; it's about being impactful so that you transcend individual goals and contribute to the greater good.

No Time Like the Present

Today marks the beginning of your journey to build your future. Every decision you make from now on should contribute to what you aspire to create for yourself and others. My advice is to focus on laying a solid foundation rather than going for quick gains through shortcuts like stock trading. Think about the long-term aspects of your life: how you plan to raise your children, what quality of life do you hope to provide for your family, what are the experiences you want to share with a partner, and what legacy do you aim to leave behind?

As a father, I've learned firsthand the dedication it takes to raise a child right. My son will need tens of thousands of hours of guidance from me to grow into a well-rounded individual. If you want to build something of significance, no matter what it is, you need to invest time and energy into creating strong, supportive relationships and a healthy environment.

So, start today. Make choices that add lasting value to your life and the lives of those around you. Embrace the idea that achievement comes from a team effort and a clear vision of your goals. By doing so, you increase the chances that your journey is not only successful, but fulfilling and enriching for you and your loved ones.

Overcoming Challenges in Education

Starting projects aimed at creating a better future has been the central theme in my effort to contribute to society. My journey started with the nonprofit aimed at reaching as many communities as possible with a powerful new approach to education and personal development. We created a mentorship program that used experiential learning, belief intelligence, and structured frameworks proven to cause growth and empowerment in students.

The objective was simple: provide support to those affected by bullying and to cause positive, long-lasting change in communities. This would nurture the next generation.

However, we soon found that the schools we worked with lacked continuity when it came to leadership, which we needed in order to cause long-lasting change. A principal would retire or a superintendent would change positions, and our whole program was usually derailed. We were relying too much on things out of our control. Not a great business model for building significance and sustainability. We needed to create our own operations, as was suggested to me. I agreed.

By founding our own schools, we have been able to implement a sustainable educational model rooted in belief intelligence, emotional intelligence, and the development of independent, rational thinkers with a passion to learn. These foundational elements are critical in building a culture that not only teaches academics but also prepares students to handle the ups and downs of life with confidence and self-awareness.

Starting these schools allowed us to lay down permanent building blocks for an educational system that could stand the test of time, free from the problems caused by changing administrations or bad policies. This approach has changed the landscape of education in the communities we serve. It has created a sturdy platform for consistent growth in young minds. They are learning to be thoughtful, well-rounded, and capable individuals in the future.

In high school, I was taught that Christopher Columbus discovered America, a claim that made its way into countless history books despite being factually incorrect. Columbus never set foot in what is now known as the United States of America; instead, he landed in the Bahamas and other parts of the Caribbean. This example reveals a bigger problem with historical "facts": the winners write history[3]. They have the power to omit, change, or completely rewrite events to fit their agendas, which shapes the public's perception over generations.

This manipulation shows why it's crucial for future generations to think independently. We need to encourage young people to question the information presented to them, to research thoroughly, and to critically evaluate the validity of

---

3   As per the Gilder Lehrman Institute of American History.

claims they find in books or online. By doing so, they can develop informed beliefs that they can translate into significance.

One of the main goals of our education system is to foster this type of critical thinking. We aim to teach individuals who are not only knowledgeable but also know how to analyze and think independently. A society where people just accept what they're told is not meant to last. The society in which civilians actively engage with and question the world around them, leading to more informed and effective actions, is the one that is built to succeed.

The Future of Foundation Academies

Our company has diversified. We currently own a branding agency, a security firm, a health company, a private school district, an online education platform, and a communication network named puder.ai. Our goal is to launch schools worldwide, including in India, Central and South America, Africa, and Europe. This global network will enable us to connect students internationally, offering them broader perspectives and greater opportunities. This improves their chances at making impactful contributions for future generations.

Looking ahead, the outlook for education is promising, thanks to technological advancements. The use of augmented reality, artificial intelligence, and machine learning signals a new, cutting-edge era in learning. This tech will revolutionize how educational content is delivered, making learning more accessible, engaging, and effective. We at Foundation Academies are committed to shaping this future; our students will benefit from the most innovative and effective educational tools. This approach to education allows us to prepare young minds to meet the challenges of tomorrow with knowledge and confidence.

My dream is to revolutionize education by creating specialized trade schools within our existing school systems. Our students won't have to attend traditional colleges for vocational training. Imagine a Yacht Academy in South Florida, where young people who aspire to have careers at sea can learn everything about navigating yachts and managing maritime logistics, or a Medical Academy for students who want to start work the day they turn 18 in a medical field, with their certificates already completed. This is part of my vision to develop a school system that not only educates millions of kids, but also inspires teachers, parents, and communities to rethink the framework of education. We'd be showing them a newer, better way of doing things.

I envision school districts embracing new technologies like artificial intelligence, augmented reality, and machine learning. These tools can dramatically enhance how students learn, for they make learning more interactive and tailored to individual needs. This provides our children with the finest education possible.

Realizing such a vision requires a committed team, and I am fortunate to work with partners and staff who are truly exceptional. They are deeply invested in the success of our projects for the benefit of future generations. Building a team-oriented culture in our organization has not been without its challenges. We face hurdles just like any company does. We have to navigate through different opinions and disagreements. However, these different ideas also bring fresh perspectives to the table, which improves our discussions and helps us to mold better strategies for achieving our goals.

Effective teamwork means appreciating these different viewpoints and finding ways to use them when appropriate. It's rare for a team to be in complete agreement, but the strength of our group is our ability to resolve conflicts and unite around our common purpose. This relationship is extremely important as we continue trying to transform education and improve young minds in a rapidly changing world.

Creating a team in life is crucial for taking a vision and turning it into a reality. The bigger the vision, the more people it requires to achieve the best outcome. My business partners have been instrumental in this process, each bringing their unique skills, perspectives, and personal touches. This diversity helps us grow personally and professionally.

We have some very ambitious goals. One of our major objectives by the year 2029 is to establish 100 schools across the United States and expand internationally. This is not just a numbers game. It's also about learning from different cultures and educational systems in order to build the best possible learning environment for future generations of other countries.

By 2035, we aim to operate a thousand campuses worldwide. This vision was inspired by someone I met whose father successfully established over a thousand schools around the globe. This meeting showed me what was possible and inspired me to reach this level.

I am convinced that we can change the world—one school, one family, and one child at a time. Each new school is a step towards giving more children the opportunity to lead significant and impactful lives. This is not just a dream; it's a plan in action, driven by a dedicated team committed to making a lasting difference in the world.

Puder.ai is designed to revolutionize how we connect and educate the world, using the latest in artificial intelligence, machine learning, and augmented reality. Within the next 5 to 10 years, AI is expected to become a household tool, dramatically enhancing the schooling experience by giving families and educators data-driven insights into a student's strengths, weaknesses, and learning style.

The primary goal of puder.ai is to establish a transparent platform that simplifies and improves the classroom experience. By building the right systems and processes, we can make schools more competitive and efficient. This platform will tailor educational content to match students' learning styles, love languages, biofeedback markers, and emerging technologies specifically developed for education.

As I touched upon, our vision for schools of the future also includes an emphasis in practical trade skills in the curriculum. Students will have the opportunity to learn trades and professions like assistant nurse practitioner, phlebotomist,

911 call center operator, engineer, yacht captain, security guard, IT technician, and air conditioning engineer, among others. Education is no longer just about the traditional core curriculum, taught by teaching talking to students for eight hours per day. It's also about preparing students for real world careers and challenges.

Puder.ai is more than just a technological tool; it represents the future of education. It arms the next generation with the skills, knowledge, and adaptability they need to thrive in a rapidly changing world.

Puder's Journal on Time to Build

I want you to take some time to think about what you've already built. It doesn't matter how big or small it is; everyone has developed something in their lives. Now, how are we going to develop this thing?

After you're done patting yourself on the back over what is, let's focus on what will be. A vision board is a good tool to use for this exercise, but I challenge you to put pen to paper here and write out how you're going to build something to positively affect both your life and the lives of others. I believe in you, dream big here. You and I both know there will be challenges no matter what you write. Let's shoot for the stars!

What have you built already?

_____

_____

_____

_____

_____

_____

What will you build in the future?

_____

_____

_____

_____

_____

_____

_____

Chapter 11: Significance Develops Legacy

People don't usually start thinking about their legacy until later on in life—typically during their 50s, 60s, or 70s. Ideas of what a meaningful legacy actually is can vary a lot. Some people disregard the idea entirely, choosing to focus on the here instead. They argue that legacy is irrelevant because they won't be around to appreciate it anyway. Best to worry about the immediate impact of your thoughts and actions. The stuff you'll see the effect of while you're still on this Earth. This perspective is valid, but it is very different from mine.

For me, the significance of legacy is not about personal fame or leaving behind a vast empire for future generations to inherit. Instead, it's about making a positive impact on the world and improving it in whatever way I can as one person. Today's global challenges are daunting, from environmental issues, to social inequalities, to ongoing international conflicts, to deep-seated hatred in our own country. These problems call for meaningful contributions from everyone in order to solve them. That's how we create a better, more sustainable world. It's our duty to take care of this one Earth we call home.

My goal is to leave behind something of real value—not necessarily in the form of material wealth or business success, but a platform that future generations can use to make a difference. While my son, Konrad, and any potential future children I have might not choose to follow directly in my footsteps, I hope I teach them the importance of creating significance in whatever field they choose. Something to make the world even a slightly better place.

Konrad's character is a constant source of inspiration for me. The joy he has, even in the face of challenges, shows me he has a strong, positive spirit. For instance, most of the time, no matter if he's feeling under the weather or just having a tough day, his attitude remains remarkably positive. When we ask him how he's doing, he always responds with optimism. It reminds me a lot of my late grandmother. Her ability to remain cheerful and strong, regardless of circumstances, has greatly influenced my understanding of what it means to live a meaningful life. Konrad gives off the same energy as her.

My view on legacy is deeply rooted in the belief that our actions should create lasting, positive change. It's about creating an environment where the next generation can succeed and continue a cycle of improvement. By building a company based on strong values and a commitment to making a difference, I hope to leave a legacy that goes beyond materialistic things. It is about making a better future through deliberate, thoughtful actions that address today's needs and pave the way for a better tomorrow.

The following section will be addressed directly to Konrad, who will be turning four years old later in 2024.

Dear Konrad,

This letter is in one of the first books I've published. It's focused on an idea I love called "Significance Breeds Success." As you grow, you'll encounter many choices and paths in life. With the guidance from me, your mom, our family, and mentors— some of whom have been pivotal in my life and will hopefully add value to yours too—I trust you'll navigate these decisions well.

From the moment you arrived in this world, your actions and the way you live your life has impressed me. At just three years old, your burning love of life, whether you're playing with monster trucks or running the beach, shows the pure joy and significance these moments hold. It's these experiences, whether when you're playing or faced with a challenge, that will shape the person you will become.

Life is a lot like training in a gym. Regular exercise strengthens the body, just as nurturing your mind, heart, spirit, and body enhances your whole being. Already, you are actively engaging in learning and sports. This will be a strong foundation for your character and abilities.

How you respond to challenges and how you stand during tough times will define your character. Developing resilience is like the training of a warrior, one who fights not just for personal gain but for the betterment of those around him. Your journey through life should be lined with significant actions that not only focus on achieving your own goals, but also on creating a positive impact for your community.

Being significant means embracing a vision that goes beyond the present, and true success involves kindness, authenticity, and vulnerability. This allows you to show your true strength and character to the world.

My hope for you, my son, is that you live a life that is full and complete. Chase your dreams with as much energy as you can. Craft a huge vision for yourself, your family, and your ventures. The biggest one you can! Embrace this path with the heart of a learner and the courage of a leader. Engage with the world in ways that challenge you to grow and adapt. Each interaction, each decision, each moment you spend pursuing these goals should be rooted in significance.

In building your life around these principles, you'll not only achieve personal fulfillment and happiness but also create a legacy that will last many generations. The significance of his legacy will come not from the trophies or awards or fortunes you gain, but by the lives you touch and the positive changes you create in your community and beyond.

Always remember, Konrad, to live each day to its fullest potential. Strive not just for success but for significance. This will give you a rich, rewarding life and allow you to leave an indelible mark on the world.

I knew mom and I were going to have you. I told her. At first, she was skeptical, but a few weeks later, she woke me early in the morning, confirming that indeed, she was pregnant. I felt incredibly blessed, believing I had witnessed your spirit beginning its journey to meet us.

In the months before you were born, your mom and I would take these long beach walks. We wanted to savor the calm before our lives changed forever. We cherished every ultrasound, even the one where you seemed to be flicking us off! We both laughed. That was a memorable day.

Bringing you home from the hospital was the start of a series of firsts for us, including some...interesting ones...like changing your diaper for the first time. That moment was huge for me, believe it or not. It represented the beginning of my hands-on role in your day-to-day care. I remember dodging a few of your "surprises" during these diaper changes. You managed to get your mom, though, which was a hilarious scene for both of us (more so for me).

Since I couldn't feed you like your mom, I found a ton of joy in the other ways I could take care of you, like giving you a bath, dressing you, and ensuring you were comfortable and loved. These early days were full of both challenges and laughter. They were precious.

Each of these moments enriched my life more than you'll ever know until you have kids of your own some day. They taught me about the deep, unconditional love of a parent. Watching you grow each day has been a privilege, and I cherish every moment, knowing that these are the building blocks of your life.

Throughout my life, I've taken almost every opportunity to travel. In recent years, we've gone on around 15 to 20 trips across the U.S. We even ventured to Portugal, which was an awesome international journey. I've always believed traveling offers new perspectives, and I wanted you to experience this for yourself, even if you might've been too young to full appreciate it. You've had the chance to visit various cities and meet influential figures like Dr. Oz, Mike Tyson, and Jeff Hoffman, who have all made significant impacts in their fields.

These experiences are not just for fun. They are also geared towards your personal growth. They've given you a glimpse into a world that few have the privilege to see. I hope these experiences help shape how you might one day choose to raise your own family.

We've also explored many museums and lounged on different beaches. You've been a very good travel companion, often sleeping through flights while other children might struggle. Your calm demeanor on planes has gotten a ton of compliments from passengers and staff members. You've also loved every method of transportation, from big planes, to trucks and cars. You do seem to love your vehicles, as I see every time we go to a monster truck show or Paw Patrol event. Nowadays, in 2024, these two things are your biggest passions, especially monster trucks. We like to make ramps at home to see how they jump, flip, and land. We turn our living room into a miniature monster truck stadium.

You also love our boating trips, where you usually relax to the point of napping, and our beach visits in Miami, where we launch our boat into the ocean. These simple moments when I get to watch you interact with the world that you're only beginning to understand, are very meaningful for me. They may seem like small moments now, but for me, they are the essence of what makes a life significant. These experiences are about more than just seeing new places; they're about spending quality time together, creating lasting memories, and the joy of being in each other's company.

When I first started my journey in the business world, I was fueled by a passion for hard work and the satisfaction of getting results. Today, my motivation comes from a deeper place. It's not just about personal success, but about fulfilling my purpose to make the world a better place. I have three *main goals now: first, to have a positive impact through the companies we develop; second, to strive to be the best version of myself; and third, to guide you, Konrad, in growing into the best version of yourself.*

As I finish this chapter on "Significance Develops Legacy," I want to express how much these past three-plus years with you have meant to me. They have been the most rewarding and happy years of my life. Thank you, Konrad, for simply being you, and for the love you share with me and your mom.

Poppa

Puder's Journal of Significance Develops Legacy

My challenge for you is to determine what you want to leave behind. If you want to go even deeper, you can write down what you hope will be written on your tombstone one day. I know it might sound morbid to think about these things, but when you acknowledge the fact that you will not be here forever and that you have the power to be significant for a long time after that, it becomes a good thing to ponder and plan for. Define the significance that will define your legacy.

What do you want your legacy to be?

_____

_____

_____

_____

_____

_____

_____

_____

What do you want to be written on your tombstone?

_____

_____

_____

_____

_____

_____

_____

Chapter 12: What Education Doesn't Teach You

What is education? In the American context, education sometimes means spending 8 to 10 hours a day in a structured environment. Students are expected to absorb information passively. This setup places children in classrooms filled with sometimes 30+ classmates, with a single teacher trying to manage a wide range of needs and learning styles. Does this sound ideal to you? It never has for me. I don't find it surprising then, that the U.S. ranked #26 in math out of the 91 nations that participated in the most recent Programme for International Student Assessment (PISA). We were #6 in reading and #10 in science.[4] I think the traditional American educational model has a ton of inefficiencies that can and should be improved on immediately.

One major issue is the idea that children should "sit down, be quiet, and listen," which prioritizes obedience over engagement and critical thinking. There's also a strong push towards preparing students for a workforce that is becoming increasingly automated. As machines and AI take over more

---

[4]   As per the National Center for Education Statistics.

jobs, the skills being taught in schools are becoming more and more worthless. They are not in line with the future of the workplace. To make matters worse, there's the notion that a college degree is some magic solution to career success, despite the availability of huge amounts of educational content online. Students can likely learn most, if not all, of the content they are taught in an undergraduate program for free. I believe that broad academic education does not ensure that a person gains employment after he or she is finished with school, not as much as specialized training done in trade schools.

This approach to education has serious consequences. Based on a 2023 survey of 1,000 college graduates, less than half of them have careers that are related to the degree they received.[5] There is clearly a disconnect between educational outcomes and job market realities. This situation calls for a fresh perspective on what education should mean and how it should be delivered.

It's critical for students to understand their learning preferences and to seek out systems that align with their personal and professional goals. For those unsure of their direction post-high school, they should explore various interests rather than rush into academic or career paths that might not end up being good for them.

The U.S. military offers an interesting model through its ASVAB test, which points recruits in the career direction that fits their skills and preferences. Most military personnel are not in combat roles, but support positions that are important to the operation on the back end, such as mechanics, cooks, and logistics officers. The armed forces gives people valuable training in skill acquisition within a structured environment, all without the insane costs of college.

My Vision

In response to these challenges, my vision involves reimagining education in order to serve future generations. I

---

5   Study was conducted by Next Gen Personal Finance.

am a huge supporter of trade schools within traditional school settings. This is somewhat of a best-of-both-worlds scenario, as it allows students to simultaneously acquire practical trade skills and their traditional core academic education. Specialized academies accomplish this goal, while I also think schools focused on entrepreneurship would be tremendous for the growth of our nation's youth.

My goal is to establish educational frameworks that embrace technology and innovation. Schools like ours are leveraging artificial intelligence, machine learning, and augmented reality to enhance learning experiences and make education more interactive and effective. By adopting these technologies, we can create a system that is transparent, adaptable, and directly tied to each student's needs and aspirations. Below is a basic breakdown of what this tech offers us:

1. AI algorithms can analyze student performance data and tailor learning materials to individual learning styles and pace.

2. Augmented reality can be incorporated into lessons to create immersive learning experiences.

3. Machine learning algorithms can be used as assessment tools to adjust the difficulty of questions based on a student's demonstrated knowledge.

Ultimately, building an effective educational system is about more than transferring knowledge to students more effectively. It's also about creating an environment that encourages critical thinking and prepares students for a range of life's scenarios. By creating a culture that values lifelong learning and practical skill acquisition, we can help our children be equipped to not just succeed in a career right out of high school, but to thrive in all aspects of their lives. This is the legacy I aim to build—a legacy that goes way beyond traditional learning and gives the next generation the tools they need to shape a better world.

The educational systems in some European countries present an intriguing contrast to those in the United States, particularly in their approach to early education. In some Eastern European countries, children don't begin formal education in subjects like math, science, and history until they are seven. Even after starting these subjects, there remains a significant emphasis on play and holistic human development. We start much earlier and more aggressively in the U.S., though I'm not sure this leads to better results, as many studies say otherwise.

In my own experience, like many other young people born with a ton of natural energy, the lack of an outlet for physical activity was a major challenge. Instead of using their hyperness for something constructive, these kids are often put on medication and encouraged to remain seated and quiet throughout the school day. This approach not only represses physical energy, which is supposed to be a good thing, but also hurts a child's emotional and intellectual growth.

Core curriculum in schools should prioritize life skills and soft skills that are key for personal and professional development. Things like sewing, basic car maintenance, plumbing, construction, and gardening are neglected. Additionally, financial literacy—an essential part of any adult's life—rarely gets the attention it deserves. Students should leave high school with at least a basic understanding of how to manage finances, understand credit scores, and read simple contracts. These are skills that empower students to navigate many of the complexities of the real world.

Another notable difference in educational and societal structure can be seen in the use of credit scores, or lack thereof. Only a few countries, including the U.S., Germany, Australia, and the United Kingdom, use credit scores. In contrast, when I was in Portugal, the banking system focused more on an individual's employment stability and income than on a numerical credit score. This system supports individuals on a more holistic level, rather than penalizing them for financial mistakes the made in the past, sometimes 20 or 30 years ago. In the U.S., despite our reliance on credit scores, there is a lack of education on how to manage and improve them. This has contributed to our national debt crisis; our total credit card debt exceeds $1.1 trillion.

Teaching financial literacy, understanding economic principles like inflation and how it affects wages, and initiating a better understanding of money should be a major part of education. For example, whenever minimum wage increases, there is a direct impact on the cost of goods and services. Many people don't understand that a wage increase can lead to higher prices for consumers. A basic hamburger that used to cost $5 might now cost $6 or more, for example. It would be great if a generation of students would understand these sorts of things, so they can make more fiscally responsible decisions. In order to do that, our systems need to change.

Mixing life skills with traditional learning can create a more all-encompassing educational system that not only prepares students for good careers, but also equips them to better handle life's everyday challenges. By copying some of the educational practices from certain European countries, we can enhance our system in order to prepare the next generation of civilians for the rapidly changing modern world.

The Power of Puder.ai

Education has evolved dramatically over the centuries. Today, we stand on the brink of a digital revolution in education, where traditional classrooms are filled with cutting-edge technology that offers new ways to engage and educate students.

Digital platforms have the potential to make education more inclusive by providing additional resources and flexibility for learners, although challenges remain in ensuring equitable access for all individuals. Platforms like puder.ai represent the forefront of this evolution. Its purpose is not just to deliver content to our at-risk youth, but also about teaching them how to learn independently. These techniques prepare students not just for exams, but for lifelong learning, equipping them with the skills they need to adapt and thrive in different environments.

These skills transfer very well to a professional setting. In these spaces, the ability to adapt, learn, and innovate is highly valued. Companies that succeed are often those that create an environment of continuous learning and mentorship. Good leaders and mentors can make a significant difference in young professionals' careers by helping them navigate through challenges and grow in their roles.

The role of technology in education goes way past simplifying learning. For non-native English speakers, like many Foundation Academies students are, technology gives them unprecedented support. Traditional methods used to separate these students into English as a Second Language (ESL) programs, which would sometimes slow their academic progress. Modern educational platforms can serve them their core academic content in their native languages, while enhancing their English proficiency at the same time in a separate course at their disposal. This method promotes better and faster learning, helping students succeed in all subjects without language barriers.

Embracing the Future

Looking to the future, the concept of education through direct knowledge downloads, as futuristic as it sounds, might become a reality. This could transform the very nature of learning, making it faster and more efficient than most of us can imagine. Think of a world where students can download complex mathematical theories or historical facts in minutes, freeing up time for critical thinking, problem-solving, creative endeavors, and project-based learning. It's wild stuff. But it might be a major part of the future.

The shift towards project-based learning and practical skill application in education is very real, and it's something Foundation Academies plans to be at the forefront of. As knowledge becomes more accessible, the value of hands-on, practical experience will increase. Educators will need to adapt, becoming facilitators who guide students through real-world applications of their knowledge. This approach not only makes learning more engaging, but also more relevant to the needs of modern society.

The future of education looks promising, but requires big adjustments from educators and students. As we introduce more technology into learning, we need to be sure it improves education without getting rid of the human elements of teaching, such as empathy. If we do things right, though, these changes will get students ready for their careers at an early age, as well as a life of meaningful, continuous learning. A life of significance. And you know what significance breeds, don't you?

The impact of technology on education has been enormous, and it will only get bigger. It will revolutionize how we learn and teach, making knowledge more accessible. It will also call for greater responsibility in how it's applied. As students and educators, our challenge is not just to use technology to improve learning, but use it to enhance our understanding and expand our capabilities as humans in general.

Looking ahead, the future is shaped by our actions today. The decisions we make about using technology in education will determine how much it improves our lives and the lives of our children and grandchildren. It's important to look at technology not just as an efficiency tool, but as a gateway to deeper learning and more substantial human interactions.

I challenge you to reflect on the role technology plays in your life. Consider how it can contribute not just to your personal success, but to the broader goal of making the world a better place. That being said, you should understand that it's healthy to spend some time away from it as well. Embrace the opportunities you get to disconnect from digital distractions for a while. Reconnect with yourself and your community. Take time to explore new interests and develop your skills in meaningful ways.

Life is a journey filled with highs and lows, joys and challenges. Each experience is a chance to grow and define your path. Remember, you only get one life—make it count. Strive to live intentionally and leave a legacy of significance. By focusing on being the best version of yourself and positively impacting those around you, together we can create a more significant world, and with that, a more successful one too.

Puder's Journal on What Education Doesn't Teach You

If you can Google pretty much everything you can or will learn in life, then the world of information is at your fingertips. What Google might not be able to tell you is how you want to learn. I challenge you to look at how you want to learn and how you want to be part of the future of the world's education systems, if you choose to be significant in this field.

I'd also recommend looking for really good mentors in life that are in education or whichever field you want to go into.

If you don't know where to begin, simply go the social media route (I recommend LinkedIn and/or Instagram) and start searching for relevant hashtags or keywords. Find out which people are being the most significant, then shoot your shot! Offer a way they can improve their business by using you. Ask them an industry-specific question (remember there's no such thing as a stupid question). Build relationships. Get yourself out there!

What is your learning style? How do you make this work?

_____

_____

_____

_____

_____

_____

_____

_____

Which potential mentors will you be reaching out to?

_____

_____

_____

_____

_____

_____

_____

_____

Afterword

"We are what we decide to do" are words that never rang truer for me. As the youngest heavyweight champion of all time, I have become many things because of what I decided to do. I became a successful boxer because of the things I decided to do. The discipline. The sacrifice. The commitment. The conviction. All in order to make my dreams a reality. Although I have made my share of public mistakes over the years, I have decided to do better. That is why I am here now, with a beautiful family and businesses that bring me great joy.

Service to others has always been a part of my life's mission and this is something I share in common with Daniel Puder. He wakes up every day and decides to do better. I am confident Daniel's tenacious work to help children succeed is just scratching the surface for what he will accomplish in his life.

Daniel is a visionary and isn't limited by the mindset many have, which blocks them from reaching their greatest potential. I believe life is all about making your dreams into reality. I would never have been successful had I believed the people who thought I wouldn't amount to anything. Thankfully, I had a mentor, and he taught me that anything is possible if you put in the hard work, combined with belief. Daniel shares this approach. He is teaching youth to turn their disadvantages into advantages by setting up positive structures and finding mentors who help them make good decisions. This will lead to them doing great things in their lives, despite their current circumstances.

Daniel has opened many schools across the country. We opened our first school together in Arizona, called Tyson's Transformational Technologies Academy (TTA). This school will help hundreds of young people in the area who have had to deal with an extra level of adversity. Some of these kids are from broken homes, or were flunking out of their old schools, or are even victims of abuse. They need a fresh start in the classroom and in life, and with Dan and I coming together to start TTA, they are getting that chance. This is how we are creating our significance, and I know the students of TTA will experience all the amazing benefits in their lives.

The messages throughout Daniel's book are designed to create significance for a lifetime. Whether it's in a personal or professional setting, the focus should always center around being significant and making a difference, which will have an impact on the lives of others around you. As long as you make the decision every day to do better, you will be better.

With a positive attitude, actions and purpose, the life you want is within your reach.

- Mike Tyson, Entrepreneur and former WBA, WBC and IBF Heavyweight World Champion

COLLEGE of WILLIAM & MARY CITED PUBLICATIONS

The findings within the current study provide implications for including EI training into standard police training, especially for law enforcement officers working with juveniles. Our results align with the findings of Herz (2001) and Romosiou et al. (2018) that training programs for police officers help participants develop novel skills when targeting attitudinal and behavioral change. The MLMP TLT led to a participant-described increase in taking perspectives of others, assessing emotions, and communicating effectively with youth and co-workers, all of which describe the participants' reported increase in emotional intelligence. All law enforcement officers are community-oriented and subsequently can benefit from increased emotional intelligence. However, law enforcement who serve school communities (e.g. School Resource Officers) may find the TLT trainings to be particularly applicable to their work with youth of all ages, their families, and school communities.

Further, the findings (i.e. EI, PGI, interpersonal skills, and perspective building) reported by the participants in the current study relate to those reported by Birzer's (2008), who identified the qualities African-Americans deemed trustworthy and important in police officers. Specifically, Birzer's (2008) findings revealed that when officers demonstrated dispositions such as professionalism, empathy, effective communication skills, and a sense of compassion, African-American participants perceived positive relationships with law enforcement. Subsequently, we believe the outcomes of the present study indicate that TLT promoted skills within the participants that may result in positive interactions with the culturally diverse youth they will interact with in the community and other professionals they work alongside.

The incorporation of EI training in professional development has intrapersonal and interpersonal benefits for individuals across career domains (Romosiou et al., 2018; Schutte et al.,

2013; Slaski & Cartwright, 2003; Teding van Berkhout & Malouff, 2016). For police officers in particular, there is evidence that the implementation of leadership curricula grounded in emotional and belief intelligence has specific benefits for officers' empathy, stress, and resilience (Romosiou et al., 2018). The current study's findings provide qualitative support to existing literature on the impact of emotional intelligence training for law enforcement. Participants indicated connections between emotional intelligence and key intrapersonal and interpersonal themes, such as personal growth initiative, perspective building, and interpersonal skills. Consistently, participants reported that the impact of the training was transferable to their personal and professional relationships. As a result, emotional intelligence-based training not only enhances outcomes for law enforcement, but may also have positive impacts on the students and communities for whom officers serve.

Jennifer K. Niles, Allison T. Dukes, Patrick R. Mullen, Corrinia D. Goode & Samantha K. Jensen (2022): Experiences of Law Enforcement Officers in an Emotional and Belief Intelligence Leadership Training: A Consensual Qualitative Report, Journal of Criminal Justice Education, DOI: 10.1080/10511253.2022.2131857

Programs designed to prevent substance use often focus on skills training and psychoeducation while paying less attention to wellness factors and emotional regulation (Clarke et al., 2020; Gutierrez et al., 2020). For example, school-based prevention programs emphasize processes like goal-setting rather than developing key social-emotional concepts (Springer et al., 2004). This approach has significant benefits; however, it appears in the literature that the opportunity for greater influence on ASE lies in the construct of hope and personal growth. For adolescents, the presence of hope may serve as a protective factor against risk behaviors, including substance use (Padilla-Walker et al., 2011). This is an important consideration for mental health professionals and school counselors working with adolescents individually and in school-based programming.

For individuals struggling with substance use, hope-based interventions can impact their degree of hope, creative problem-solving, motivation to pursue goals, resilience in the face of obstacles, and overall self-efficacy (Saboor et al., 2019). Therefore, one implication of our findings for substance use prevention service providers is that the use of hope-focused and personal growth interventions could amplify current approaches to substance use treatment. Helping professionals should consider adopting prevention programs that focus on or include hope and personal growth components. In schoolwide interventions, school counselors can emphasize strategies for developing students' sense of hope and PGI. Additionally, including a focus on personal growth and hope could also benefit those in recovery from substance use disorder.

Niles, J. K., Gutierrez, D., Dukes, A. T., Mullen, P. R., & Goode, C. D. (2022). Understanding the relationships between personal growth initiative, hope, and abstinence self-efficacy. The Journal of Addictions & Offender Counseling, 1–11. https://doi.org/10.1002/jaoc.12099

We set out in this study to examine the effectiveness of the GPS for SUCCESS program. We facilitated a quasi-experiment research design comparing scores of personal growth initiative and meaning in life between the treatment group and waitlist comparison group to accomplish this aim. We found that for both personal growth initiative and meaning in life the treatment group had statistically significant higher scores when compared to the comparison group. The findings provide some initial support for the effectiveness of the GPS for Success program and indicate that the program affects theoretically congruent concepts. While the findings provided promising results, more research using randomized designs with different samples is merited.

Patrick R. Mullen, Jennifer Niles, Allison Dukes & Allison Spargo (2022): An examination of the GPS for SUCCESS program, Preventing School Failure: Alternative Education for Children and Youth, DOI: 10.1080/1045988X.2022.2048627